How to Invest $50–$5,000

=HOW TO=
INVEST
$50-$5,000

Fifth Edition

NANCY DUNNAN

HarperPerennial
A Division of HarperCollins*Publishers*

This book is sold with the understanding that neither the Author nor the Publisher is engaged in rendering legal or financial services. Questions relevant to the practice of law or personal finance should be addressed to a member of those professions.

The Author and Publisher specifically disclaim any liability, loss, or risk, personal or otherwise, which is incurred as a consequence, directly or indirectly, of the use and application of any of the contents of this work.

CONTENTS

INTRODUCTION

Getting the Most for Your Money

A fool and his money is soon parted.

—English proverb

This book is intended to help you keep your money, whether you have only a few dollars or a few thousand. Most people, regardless of their income, don't know how to save or, if they do save, what to do with their money. Consequently, they and their money part ways.

Perhaps you're a new or small investor, or you have money sitting in an account somewhere earning just 2-1/2 to 4 percent. . . . Maybe you're just starting out on your first job. . . . Maybe you've saved several hundred dollars from your summer work. . . or several thousand dollars from careful budgeting. . . . You received a sudden windfall so that for the first time in your life you have a lump sum to invest. . . . You got a bonus. . . or you have a business that's taking off. . . .

Even if you have only a small amount to invest, you should start now—today; for the sooner you begin, the sooner your $50, $500, or $5,000 will grow. Think about it: If you invested $500 at the end of each year at 8 percent compounded annually, at the end of five years you would have $2,933. At the end of ten years you would have $7,243.

You too can watch your money grow through wise investment.

Sometimes small investors feel their options are limited. They're not. More than two dozen investment vehicles are described in detail in this book. We will show you how to take advantage of each one. In fact, you'll soon discover that all the financial world is wooing you and your money. Banks, brokerage firms, insurance companies, and financial planners are vying for your cash—be it $50 or $5,000. In fact, every major financial institution has a new gimmick to entice the novice as well as to hold on to the seasoned client.

REACHING YOUR GOALS—HOW SAVING CAN BE FUN

Your personal financial goals will vary throughout your life, depending upon how old you are, your income, and your interests. The best way to reach any goal is to write it down, assign it a target date, and figure out how much you need to save to accomplish your dream. Here's a fill-in worksheet you can use as a model. Add your own particular spin to it.

Goal	Total Cost	Target Date Month	Months to Go	Save Each
Degree	_____	_____	_____	_____
New car	_____	_____	_____	_____
Computer	_____	_____	_____	_____
Vacation	_____	_____	_____	_____
House	_____	_____	_____	_____
Art work	_____	_____	_____	_____
Start business	_____	_____	_____	_____

Tip: To determine the monthly amount you need to save: divide the total amount by the number of months available before your target due date. For example, if you'd like $750 to spend on next year's vacation, 12 months from now, divide $750 by 12; you'll need to stash away $62.50 each month. Put it in an interest-bearing account and you'll actually have a little bit more to spend.

We'll explain which ones are best, which ones are safest, which ones will give you the best return. You will learn that a savings account at your corner bank is not the only option for the small investor. In this handbook, we will teach you to feel comfortable moving your money around from one investment to another as your needs change, as interest rates and the economy change. The right place for your first $50 won't be the right one for your first $500 or $5,000—just look at how interest rates and inflation have changed over the years—no one investment weathers all economic storms.

Although those of us with up to $5,000 constitute the nation's largest group of investors, it's not easy to find information explaining how to tailor personal needs to specific investment instruments. Most money books address people in high-income brackets—those who can afford a financial planner to guide their every move.

This book will change all that for you. It will fill that void by covering the specific concerns of those who have a maximum of $5,000 to invest. It will tackle the fact that in today's climate no one type of investment works well all the time, that reading the changes in interest rates is crucial, that diversification will minimize financial pitfalls, and, finally, that liquidity and the ability to move assets quickly are essential in a changing economic climate.

How to Invest $50-$5,000 will carefully guide you through the maze of money vehicles, teaching you how to develop the art of smart decision making. You will learn to tackle Wall Street and your bank with confidence and self-assurance. We won't tell you which stock to buy, which bond is best, or even which bank to use, but we will show you how to analyze your options as you watch your money grow from $50 to $5,000. Cutting through the jargon and getting right down to the basic facts, *How to Invest $50-$5,000* will explain things financial so that no matter how inexperienced you are, you soon will feel comfortable deciding where to put your investment dollars.

Being a good investor, however, takes time and knowledge. But if you follow our step-by-step plan, you'll soon know exactly what to do and when. Make a point of setting aside some time to learn about handling your money, to explore the world of finance. It's worth the time and effort for one simple reason: No one cares as much about your money as you do!

Begin by reading the box that follows called "The Ten Dumbest Mistakes People Make About Money." You'll soon see you're not alone in shying away from investing, in putting off saving. Second, put a check next to those mistakes that are yours. Third, reread the suggested solutions for each mistake. They are simple and easy to follow. Fourth and finally, resolve to take action today—or at least before the end of the month!

THE TEN DUMBEST MISTAKES PEOPLE MAKE ABOUT MONEY

1) Being ashamed to invest small amounts. With this attitude, you'll never save anything. What is small to one investor may be huge to another. **Solution:** Begin saving something from the next income or salary check you receive. The dollar amount is not important. Developing the habit of saving is. Read "Nine Easy/Painless Ways To Save" in the Appendix.

2) Having inadequate emergency savings. **Solution:** Stash three to six months' worth of living expenses in a money market mutual fund or interest-bearing checking account. Read Chapters 4 and 5.

3) Leaving cash in a regular bank savings account. **Solution:** Move it immediately to a money market fund or a money market deposit account. Read Chapters 5 and 6.

4) Operating too many accounts. If you have several bank, mutual fund, and brokerage accounts you're spending too much on service fees. And it's hard to keep track of interest rates and other details. **Solution:** Consolidate. Have one checking account, one or two money market funds and brokerage accounts.

5) Not knowing whether an investment is for current income or for appreciation. In general, a growth stock or growth mutual fund should not be expected to pay high current

---

income while a CD, bond, or utility stock should not be purchased in anticipation of price appreciation. **Solution:** Read Chapters 13 and 17.

6) Avoiding financial goals. Yogi Berra said it best: "If you don't know where you're going, you're probably going to wind up someplace else." Most people spend more time planning their vacations than their financial future. Consequently, they spend as much or more on cruises, airline tickets, and hotels than they do funding their retirement accounts or building up a nest egg. **Solution:** Develop one or two specific financial goals. Write them down or discuss them with a stockbroker or financial advisor. Preferably, do both.

7) Failing to diversify. People often put all their money in one place because it's convenient, it's familiar, or they're just plain lazy. No investment is sufficiently profitable or safe to justify this approach. **Solution:** Divide your assets among banks, mutual funds, stocks, bonds, Treasuries, and real estate.

8) Procrastinating. People put off making financial decisions because they're afraid they'll do the wrong thing. **Solution:** Set time deadlines and take several small, conservative investment steps, one at a time. For example, if you have $3,000, in week number one, put one-third into a money market account. The next week, buy a CD. The following week, use the rest to buy shares of a blue chip stock.

9) Ignoring savings plans at work. Tax-deferred plans, such as 401(k) or stock purchase plans, are usually good deals, especially if the company matches your contribution. **Solution:** Talk to your benefits officer this week. Read Chapter 11 and "Painless Ways to Save" in the Appendix.

10) Failing to have a will. Estate planning is critical if you care about other people. **Solution:** Write your will this weekend.

THE 72 RULE

A quick way to calculate how long it will take you to double your investment—at any interest rate—is to use "The 72 Rule."

Divide 72 by the interest rate and you get the number of years it will take to double your money.

For example: 72 divided by 3-1/2 percent is 24 years

72 divided by 6 percent is 12-1/2 years

Note: "The 72 rule" applies only when interest and dividends are reinvested. It does not take taxes into consideration.

How to Invest
$50–$5,000

PART ONE

Safe Stashing for Your First $50

1

Institutional Cookie Jars: Banks

In your great-grandmother's day, the family savings were often tucked away in a cookie jar, stuffed under the mattress, or hidden in a deep hole behind the back porch. People who lost money when many of the banks closed their doors in 1929, put their faith and their money in the land, just as Scarlett O'Hara's daddy advised.

Yet for most of us, a savings account at the local bank still seems the most logical holding spot for that first $50. But not necessarily. Let's take a look at what your bank will do with your $50 and what other options you have.

Selecting a Bank

Not all banks treat all customers equally. So, don't make a mad dash to the first bank on your corner. It pays to shop around, even with only $50 burning a hole in your pocket. Eventually you will become a larger depositor and will need to use the bank for other reasons—a loan, a mortgage, or a checking account. Some banks offer estate planning, courses in financial planning, mutual funds, computerized investing—all services you may want later on.

Since most Americans are always in a hurry, the single most common factor in deciding where to bank is, of course, location. Yet, your nearest bank is not necessarily the right choice for you. Before opening a savings account, check out your neighborhood bank, by all means, but also make personal visits to several others. At each one make an appointment with the person in charge of new accounts. Describe your financial needs; see what the advisor suggests. Don't worry about the quality of the wall-to-wall carpeting or the abundance of fresh flowers. Decor is, of course, not the issue. But other things certainly are.

Check to see:

- What the minimum deposit requirement is for a savings account
- If all types of services are offered
- How well rush-hour traffic is handled
- If there are express lines
- If there are branches near both where you live and where you work
- If there are bank officers available to answer questions, or if you are likely to be sent scurrying from one desk to another in a Kafkalike circle
- If there is written material available on interest rates and service charges—material that you can actually understand
- Then, compare fees and interest rates of all the banks you visit

And, check out **credit unions**.

Credit unions emerged in this country in the early 1900s to help those working class people who didn't qualify for loans from commercial banks. The members of a credit union pooled their money and made low-interest loans to one another. Today credit unions serve those people with a common bond (see Chapter 2 for more on these institutions). Although banks are free to pay whatever rate they choose, as of late 1994 they were paying 1.8 to 3.5 percent on savings accounts. Credit unions were paying around 3 percent.

The stated rate, however, is only the tip of the iceberg. It is also important to know exactly how often the interest will be paid, because every time your account is credited with interest, you will have that much more money to calculate on the next time interest is paid. In other words, the more frequently interest is **compounded**, the more money you will earn.

So, open your account at a bank where interest is compounded daily; it will provide a better return than if interest is compounded quarterly.

Passbook and Savings Accounts

If you have a small amount to invest, you'll obviously need to begin with a bank that will accept your deposit. In a small-town bank it may be only $5, while a larger bank may require $100 or more.

Historically, banks offered two types of savings accounts: **passbook accounts** and monthly **statement accounts**. Although many have done away with the passbook type, there are still plenty around. Savers receive a thin booklet in which the bank records all deposits, withdrawals, and interest payments after each transaction. You take the book to the bank each time you put in or take out money. With a statement account you do not have a booklet. Instead you receive a printed monthly statement detailing all transactions. Its advantage: You do not have to worry about losing your passbook.

Most banks have either a passbook or a statement type account and do not give you a choice. Some, however, have both, paying slightly different interest rates on each. Be certain to ask if the bank offers both and what the rates are on each.

Fees

In many banks, if your balance falls below a certain amount, you will be assessed a monthly charge or you will lose interest, or possibly both. For example, a bank may require a $500 minimum to open a statement savings account, on which it will pay 3.5 percent, but if your balance falls below $500, a monthly fee of $1.50 is slapped on. So you could actually lose money because of the monthly charge! Or the bank may have a passbook savings account, available for as little as $5, but it pays only 2.5 percent. Check these details carefully when selecting a bank for your first $50. And remember, if your account is inactive, meaning you have not made a deposit or withdrawal during a certain time period, banks typically charge a small monthly fee.

Yield

Banks often advertise two figures: the annual interest rate and the effective yield. The difference between the two comes from how often interest is credited to your balance, thus increasing the principal on which interest is paid. A 3 percent interest rate has an effective annual yield of 3 percent if the interest is credited annually. If it is credited quarterly, the effective yield is 3.094 percent, and if interest is credited monthly, the effective yield is 3.116 percent.

BANK SAVINGS ACCOUNT

For Whom

- Small savers
- Those with less than $500

4

Where to Open

- Bank
- Savings and loan association

Fees and Minimum Balance

- No opening fee
- Monthly fees vary if balance drops below certain level

Safety Factor

- High
- Deposits insured up to $100,000 at all FDIC (Federal Deposit Insurance Corporation) insured institutions

Advantages

- Safety
- Geographically accessible
- Withdrawal upon demand, aka "liquidity"
- Principal is guaranteed up to $100,000 by federally backed insurance corporation if bank is FDIC insured
- When account is sizeable, it can often be used as collateral for a loan

Disadvantages

- Interest rate is low and fixed
- Checks cannot be written against the account
- Monthly fees on low balances may mean you will lose money

Coupon Clubs

It's certainly gimmicky, but if it helps you save, then give the bank coupon club a try.

The coupon club is the generic name for a myriad of programs devised by banks to attract business. These include Christmas clubs, Hanukkah clubs, vacation clubs, and so forth. They are also offered by many savings and loan associations and credit unions.

If you decide to join one, each week or month, depending upon the club, you will make a specified deposit or payment, enclosing a coupon with your money. At the end of a stated period, usually a year, your coupons will all be gone and your account full of money. In some clubs you cannot withdraw your money until the stated period is over.

Couponless Plans

In some banks, you can sign up for automatic savings deposit plans if you make the arrangements. You designate the monthly amount you want to save, let's say $35. This amount is then automatically taken out of your checking account and deposited into your savings account where it will earn interest. The record of your transaction is then attached to your regular checking account statement.

COUPON CLUBS

For Whom

- Undisciplined savers
- People with large families who have to buy lots of holiday gifts
- Those who like tearing along perforated lines

Fee

- Usually none

Safety

- High

Advantages

- Forced way to save

Disadvantages

- Some clubs pay low interest or no interest at all
- Some pay interest only if you complete the full term of the club
- You may not be able to withdraw your money until the full year is over

ATMs

Automated teller machines, electronic machines located in bank lobbies, shopping centers, and on street corners across America, provide instant access to money 24 hours a day. To use an ATM you need an encoded plastic card, which is inserted into the machine, and a personal identification number (PIN), issued by the bank. This PIN number is then punched in on the machine to access your account. Obviously you should never give your PIN number to another person nor have it written down in your wallet; instead pick a number that you can memorize, such as your wedding anniversary or your mother's birthday. Don't pick your own birthday—thieves are on to that one.

Although ATMs are a godsend on weekends and when bank lines are long, use them with discretion:

- Check to see whether your bank charges for each ATM transaction.
- Very often cards issued by one bank may be used in the ATM of another bank, but for a fee.
- Use a bank that is part of an ATM network, such as MAC, MOST, NYCE, SAM, STAR, or CIRRUS, in which case you can use your ATM when you're out of state or even overseas.

- Visa and MasterCard can be used in many ATMs for cash advances.

 Caution: You often pay service charges as well as interest on these advances from the minute you receive the cash.

- Time your withdrawals. If you want money from your bank's money market deposit account where it's earning interest, make your withdrawal by ATM after 3 P.M., the bank's official closing hour. That way you'll get the maximum interest.

➤**Hint:** Each bank sets a limit on how much cash you can withdraw on any one day. If you're planning to get cash for a trip, check the daily limit first.

Ways to Get the Most Out of Your Bank

New electronic systems, revised banking rules, and expanded marketing programs all mean better deals for savvy bank customers. Read the examples below and then talk to your banker. These and other "deals" are not always advertised.

- *Currency exchange.* When abroad, get an exchange rate bargain by using a bank's automated teller machine (ATM) card to purchase foreign currency. Your PLUS or CIRRUS card, issued by U.S. banks that are members of one of those ATM networks, may be used at thousands of outlets around the world to withdraw local currency. The machine dispenses currency at an exchange rate that's several percentage points less than the official retail rate. And you don't pay the added transaction cost that many banks, hotels, and others often charge for accepting U.S. dollar traveler's checks.
- *Buyer protection plan.* Goods purchased by using some bank-sponsored credit cards get an extended warranty for 60 to 90 days.
- *Senior citizens' programs.* Free checking, no-fee credit cards,

free traveler's checks, and discounts on tickets to cultural events for "older" customers.

- *Favorable loan and mortgage rates.* Banks often give preferential treatment to customers when it comes to lending money. Ask.
- *Fees waived.* Customers who combine deposits and loans and keep a minimum balance don't always have to pay service charges.

A Bank Checkup

- Ask your banker how interest is compounded.
- Get a printed chart of interest rates to study at home.
- Ask if the bank pays interest only on the lowest balance during the quarter. For example, if you have $200 in your account and you take out $75, then eventually build it back up to $200, is interest paid as though you had only $125 in the account all the time?
- Look for a bank paying interest from day of deposit to day of withdrawal.
- Will you be charged extra if you make many withdrawals?
- Are there any days at the end of the quarter when interest is not paid?
- How many days are in the bank's year? (Some banks have "dead days" at the end of a quarter when they don't pay interest.)
- If you take out money, or close the account at mid-quarter, will you lose interest?
- Are there penalties for leaving your account inactive for a long period?
- Is there a monthly service charge?

Study carefully the chart on annually compounded interest in a $50 account and use it as a guideline for making your banking decision.

$50 COMPOUNDED AT 5 PERCENT
Compounding Periods Per Year

Years	semi-annually	annually	quarterly	monthly	daily
1	$52.50	$52.53	$52.55	$52.56	$52.58
2	63.81	64.00	64.10	64.17	64.20
10	81.44	81.93	82.18	82.35	83.43
20	132.66	134.25	135.07	135.63	135.90

Source: Credit Union National Association, Inc.

How Safe Is Your Bank?

The rash of bank failures in the late 1980s has made even the most financially reckless aware of the importance of safety. There's no need to tuck your money under the mattress, but you should:

1) Bank only at federally insured institutions. Look for the FDIC sign at the bank. It stands for Federal Deposit Insurance Corporation, an independent agency of the U.S. Government that was established by Congress in 1933 to insure bank deposits. Member banks pay for the cost of insurance through semiannual assessments.

2) Keep in mind that individual depositors, not accounts, are insured—up to $100,000, including interest and principal. That means if you have two accounts in the same name in one bank, you are insured only for $100,000, not $200,000.

3) Find out how safe your bank really is. For a $10 fee, Veribanc, Inc., will send you a financial evaluation of any bank or savings and loan as well as its FDIC category: well capitalized, adequately capitalized, and undercapitalized. Contact Veribanc, Inc., at P.O. Box 461, Wakefield, MA 01880; 800-442-2657; 617-245-8370.

4) If you discover your bank is a weakling, move your money

to the strongest institution in your area. Veribanc will provide the names of such banks for a $38 fee.

➤ **Hint:** You may wish to wait until any certificates of deposit mature before transferring money so as not to lose out on any interest.

5) For information on FDIC insurance, call the consumer hotline at 800-934-3342, or write the Office of Consumer Affairs for a free copy of "Your Insured Deposit" at 550 17th Street NW, Washington, DC 20429.

2

Credit Unions

Once thought of only as a place for assembly line workers to get a car loan, **credit unions** have taken on a brand new look. They are a viable choice for your $50, and they usually pay one or two percentage points above bank rates. There is no lid on interest rates; they vary from union to union.

Credit unions are cooperatives, or not-for-profit associations of people who pool their savings and then lend money to one another. By law, they must have so-called "common bonds," which may consist in working for the same employer, belonging to the same church, club, or government agency, or even living in the same neighborhood. Because they are not-for-profit and because overhead costs are low, credit unions almost always give savers and borrowers better rates and terms than commercial institutions.

There are more than 13,000 U.S. credit unions with assets in excess of $200.5 billion. While the largest, the Navy Federal Credit Union, has about a million members, the average has 2,000.

Today's upbeat union bears very little resemblance to the cooperatives established some seventy-five years ago in order to save working-class people from the ubiquitous loan shark. These feisty cooperatives have aggressively expanded their turf, offering a line of sophisticated financial services and often competing very favorably with commercial banks and savings and loans. Many, in fact, operate like local banks.

Theoretically, unions are run by the depositors—every member, in fact, must be a depositor, albeit a very small one, although the true organizational work is done by volunteer committees in the smaller unions and by paid employees in the larger groups.

If you are not already a member of a credit union, but would like to be one, call the industry's trade organization for information on how to join or start a credit union:

Credit Union National Association, 800-358-5710

But before you invest your $50 in a credit union:

- Make sure the union is insured by the National Credit Union Share Insurance Fund, a federal agency.
- Inquire about its reputation from members.

➤ **Hint:** For a free copy of "Share a Common Interest: Sponsor a Union," write to the National Association of Federal Credit Unions, P.O. Box 3769, Washington, DC 20007.

CREDIT UNIONS

For Whom

- Members and members' families

Where to Find

- Your place of work
- Your neighborhood association
- Church, club, synagogue, YMCA, YWCA

Minimum

- You must buy at least one share to join a credit union
- Shares are determined by each union and vary from $5 to $30, with most around $15. (A share is really your first deposit.)

Safety

- Varies, but generally above average
- High if insured by National Credit Union Share Insurance Fund

Advantages

- Friendly, supportive attitude toward members
- Interest rates on savings are generally higher than at commercial institutions
- Interest rates on loans are generally lower than at commercial institutions
- Other services may be offered, such as mortgages, credit cards, checking accounts, IRAs, CDs
- An automatic payroll deduction savings plan is frequently available
- Purchase of stocks listed on the New York Stock Exchange and other exchanges is possible at low commissions at some credit unions

Disadvantages

- Might be run by inexperienced volunteers or inadequately staffed
- Might not be adequately insured
- May not return canceled checks

3

Uncle Sam & Savings Bonds

The bank isn't the only safe slow-growth investment vehicle for your $50. Uncle Sam is willing and eager to keep it for you and, in return, provide a little something in the way of interest through what is known as a **U.S. Savings Bond.** When you buy a U.S. Savings Bond you are lending money to the U.S. Government.

A few years ago, the government savings bond program was known as the dog of the investment world, paying interest rates far below average, and so low that investors could not keep up with inflation.

The program, however, was revamped, revised, and remarketed. Now the Series EE Savings Bonds are a viable way to save small amounts of money (known as preserving capital) and at the same time earn interest.

You can buy EE bonds at most banks and there's no fee. The purchase price is actually 50 percent of the bond's face value, so in other words, a $50 bond costs only $25. (EE Savings Bonds are sold in the following face value amounts: $50, $75, $100, $200, $500, $1,000, $5,000, and $10,000.) If you hold them until maturity, you'll get back the face value, $50 per bond in the case of a $25 bond, plus variable interest. In addition to buying these bonds at the bank, you may also buy them through automatic payroll deductions, as thousands of employers participate in the savings bond program. This is a good way to save if you're not a natural saver. In fact, after a while you may not even miss the amount taken from your paycheck.

EE bonds pay 4 percent for the first five years. After that, you earn interest equal to 85 percent of the average yield on five-year Treasury notes, with a minimum of 4 percent guaranteed.

🛑 *Caution:* If you cash in your bond before five years are up you won't earn the top rate of interest. You cannot, however, redeem your bond **at all** during the first six months. For the current rate on bonds held five years or more, telephone 800-US-BONDS. This rate changes each November 1 and May 1. Until May 1, 1995 that rate is 5.92 percent.

EE SAVINGS BONDS

For Whom

- Those who won't need the money until five years have passed
- Those who want a competitive deferred yield
- Those who have a low tolerance for risk and want to be certain that their principal is safe

Where to Purchase

- Banks
- Payroll savings plan
- Savings and loan associations
- Credit unions
- Federal Reserve Bank (see addresses on page 92–93)
- Bureau of the Public Debt, Securities Transaction Branch, Washington, DC 20239

Fee and Minimum

- No fee
- Minimum purchase, $25 for a $50 bond

Safety Rating

- Highest possible

Advantages

- Virtually no risk because the principal is government-backed and interest is default proof
- Easy to buy at your local bank
- No commission or sales fee

- Income is exempt from state and local taxes
- Federal tax can be deferred until bonds are redeemed or mature
- EE bonds are an excellent way to save for a child's education, especially if you can target them to come due after he or she reaches age 14, at which point the interest income will be taxed at the child's lower rate. (Until the child turns 14, however, earned investment income from assets given to the child by a parent are taxed at the parent's presumably higher rate.)
- EE bonds purchased after January 1, 1990, by a bondholder at least age 24 and used to pay college tuition are free from federal income tax provided you fall within certain income guidelines when the bonds are redeemed. Ask your local bank for details.
- Upon maturity, you may reinvest, or roll over, your Series EE Savings Bonds into Series HH bonds and further defer your taxes until the HH bonds mature, another ten years down the road. HH bonds can be purchased only by rolling over EE bonds that have reached maturity and are available in denominations of $500.

For more information on savings bonds, write:
    Office of Public Affairs
    U.S. Savings Bond Division
    Washington, DC 20226
For information on payroll savings, call:
    Payroll Savings Plan
    202-377-7715

PAYING FOR COLLEGE WITH SAVINGS BONDS

The earlier you start saving, the more you will have when your child is ready for college. This information, from the Bureau of Public Debt, assumes that you invest in EE Savings Bonds at an annual interest rate of 4 percent; the actual rate may be higher, which would affect the total saved.

Child's Age When Savings Start	Monthly Investments of $50	$100
	Will Grow to These Amounts by Age 18:	
1 year old	$14,579	$29,158
6 years old	9,233	18,466
10 years old	5,656	11,312
12 years old	4,069	8,138

4

Interest-Paying Checking Accounts

Intense competition for savers' money has forced banks to pay interest on certain types of checking accounts. You should take advantage of this situation—again by taking time to shop around for the best deal given the amount of money you regularly keep in your account.

Keep in mind that today holding cash is an investment choice—there are a number of places where you can park $500 or more, earn interest, and have fairly easy access to your money. We will discuss all five choices in this book. They are:

- Interest-paying checking accounts
- Money market mutual funds
- Insured bank money market deposit accounts
- Bank certificates of deposit (CDs)
- Treasury bills, notes, and bonds

(Note: Savings accounts and EE savings bonds are two other choices, available for those with less than $500 and so are covered in Chapters 1 and 3.)

First, let's take a look at interest-paying checking accounts, sometimes called **NOW accounts.** NOW stands for Negotiable Order of Withdrawal. These are like regular checking accounts with printed checks and regular statements, but they *also* pay interest—anywhere from 1.25 percent to 2.75 percent. They are simply a handy housekeeping account that permits you to earn a little interest on your cash balance as you pay bills. Sounds good. But there are several caveats attached. In order to earn the interest, a minimum or monthly average balance must be maintained. These minimums vary nationwide from about $500 to $2,500, sometimes as much as $3,000.

If you fall below the required minimum balance, you will lose interest and you may also be subject to per-check, per-deposit, and/or monthly charges.

The equivalent of this account at a credit union is called a **share draft.** Since credit unions do not have a cap on the amount of interest they can pay, share drafts generally offer slightly higher rates than bank accounts. (See pages 12–14 for more on credit unions.)

Before opening an interest-paying checking account, quiz your banker and get precise answers to these questions:

- How is the minimum balance determined? Most banks add up your balance at the end of each day. If you're short, even for one day, you're slapped with a full service fee.
- Avoid banks that use the *low balance* method. They look only at the lowest point in your checking account that month.
- If you fall below the minimum, what will you be charged? Banks have devised several clever ways of addressing this question. Some charge you for every check written during the month; others only for those written during the time when your account fell below minimum requirements. Another variation on the theme: You'll be charged only if you write more than a certain number of checks, say fifteen or twenty. Regardless of the methods used by the bank, it

pays to have this type of account only *if* you maintain the minimum balance.

- How is the interest figured? Again, as in a passbook savings account (see Chapter 1), you will get the best deal if your interest is figured from day of deposit to day of withdrawal, or on your daily average balance.

In the competitive banking world of today, an interest-paying checking account is a good choice *if* you can maintain the minimum amount in order to avoid having to pay steep fees and charges that eat up any earned interest. But do your calculations carefully. If you know maintaining the balance will be difficult, you will be better off with a regular checking account.

INTEREST-PAYING CHECKING ACCOUNTS

For Whom

- Ideal for anyone who wants a checking account and can maintain the bank's minimum balance at all times

Minimum

- Varies from around $500 to $2,500 or more

Safety Factor

- Insured up to $100,000

Advantages

- You can earn interest on a checking account
- You can write checks for any amount
- You may get overdraft privileges so checks don't bounce

Disadvantages

- Bank charges on regular checking accounts are almost universally lower than on these special accounts
- Minimums for maintaining accounts are steep

After you have taken care of opening your checking account, the next $500 you accumulate should be transferred to one of the higher-paying parking places where you can earn more interest than in a passbook savings account or interest-bearing checking account.

First we will examine the pros and cons of money market mutual funds and then we will move on to CDs, Treasury notes and bonds, and other high-yielding places for your money.

5

Money Market
Mutual Funds

After you've opened a checking account and accumulated an extra $500, the next step is to find a safe place to put your hard-earned savings. One choice is a **money market mutual fund** where you can earn more interest than in a regular savings or checking account.

What is a mutual fund?

To understand what a money market mutual fund is, you first need to know how mutual funds in general work. A mutual fund is actually an investment company in which you (e.g., the public) buy shares. This means that your investment dollars are pooled with those of hundreds of other investors and the combined total is invested by a professional manager in various investment vehicles—stocks, bonds, cash, etc. The fund manager studies the market, interest rates, and other economic indicators, buying and selling those investments that best suit the fund's stated aims or goals. These goals might be to achieve income, price appreciation, or tax-free returns for those in the fund. (See Chapter 13, pages 71–84 for information about purchasing mutual funds from a bank.)

The Powerful Advantage of Mutual Funds

The value of a fund is that one large pool of money can be far more effectively invested than hundreds or thousands of small sums. Each investor, no matter how large or small his or her investment, then owns a proportional share of the fund, and receives a proportional return, without discrimination based on the number of shares owned.

There are many types of funds. Some are set up for long-term growth, some for immediate income, others for tax-free returns. Some are willing to take higher levels of risk than others. Some are devoted exclusively to buying and selling stocks; others to bonds, or a combination of the two.

In the case of a money market mutual fund, the goal is a high yield with minimum risk. Money market funds derive their name from the type of securities they invest in "money market" securities.

Financial companies, large corporations, and the U.S. Government all borrow large sums of money for short periods (one year or less) by issuing **money market securities** in exchange for cash. For example, the government borrows by way of Treasury bills (T-bills) and notes; large corporations by IOUs called commercial paper; and banks by way of large certificates of deposit called jumbo CDs.

These money market securities make up the fund's portfolio, rather than stocks and bonds.

The borrowers—the government, large corporations, and banks—are good credit risks. They consist of the country's most solid institutions, and they all agree to pay back the money quickly and at high rates. That's why today you can earn more than with a traditional savings account.

Obviously no ordinary saver would be able to participate in this venture on his or her own. The amounts involved are too large. But through a money market mutual fund, the average investor can indeed share in this opportunity at relatively minimal cost. The money earned by the fund, after expenses, is in turn paid out to you, the shareholder, as interest or "dividends."

Although many funds require a minimum deposit of $1,000, with additional deposits of at least $100, there is one fund with no minimum opening requirements:

- Alger Money Market Portfolio
  800-992-3863

A key point in favor of these funds is their liquidity. You have almost immediate access to your money without penalty. You can cash in your shares by phone, by mail, or through your broker. And, most funds will wire money from the fund directly to your local bank if you so arrange in advance. Generally you can also tap the money by writing checks against your shares. Usually a fund permits unlimited check writing as long as the checks are for amounts over $500.

One fund, however, will let you write checks for as little as $100; it has an opening minimum of only $500:

- Money Market Management
  Federated Investors
  Federated Tower
  Pittsburgh, PA 15222-3779
  800-245-2423

Several funds have only $500 minimums for opening:

- Templeton Money Fund
  800-237-0738
- Oppenheimer Cash Accumulation
  800-525-9310
- Franklin Group Money Funds
  800-342-5236
- Liberty Government Money Market Trust
  800-245-4770

To invest, call or write away for a copy of each fund's prospectus. It contains an account form and also tells what investments are in the fund's portfolio along with statistics on its past performance. Money market funds and their yields are also listed in the financial pages of the newspaper.

In selecting a fund, ask yourself these questions:

- What minimum investment can I afford?
- Do I want a fund nearby, through my broker, or can I invest by telephone or by wire?

- How easily can I redeem my shares? What is the fund's policy about writing checks? Will the fund wire money to my bank? How long will it take? Is there an extra charge for this service?
- Can I transfer from this fund to another if the economic climate changes?
- What types of securities does the fund invest in? Would I feel safe in a different type of fund, say one that invests only in government securities?

There are hundreds of these money market mutual funds open to individual savers. For a directory of mutual funds, send $8.50 to:

The Investment Company Institute
1401 H Street NW
Washington, DC 20036
202-326-5800

This pamphlet contains the names, addresses, and toll-free telephone numbers as well as the initial and subsequent investment minimums of each fund.

THE HIGHEST YIELDING MONEY MARKET FUNDS

Fund	Telephone	Minimum
Fidelity Spartan	800-544-8888	$20,000
Dreyfus Worldwide Dollar Money Fund	800-645-6561	2,500
Alger Portfolio	800-992-3863	none
Evergreen Trust	800-235-0064	2,000
Flex Fund	800-325-FLEX	2,500

WHAT KINDS OF THINGS
MONEY MARKET FUNDS BUY

Agency securities. Issued by government agencies such as Government National Mortgage Association (Ginnie Mae) and the Small Business Administration or by government-sponsored organizations such as the Federal National Mortgage Association (Fannie Mae) and the Federal Home Loan Banks.

Bankers' acceptance. Commercial notes guaranteed by a bank.

Certificates of deposit. Large-denomination, negotiable CDs sold by both U.S. and foreign commercial banks and by some S&Ls.

Commercial paper. IOUs sold by corporations for day-to-day operating funds.

Eurodollar CDs. Dollar-denominated certificates sold by foreign branches of U.S. banks or by foreign banks.

Treasury bills and notes. Sold on a periodic basis by the U.S. Treasury and backed by the "full faith and credit" of the government.

Repurchase agreements. "Repros," buy-sell deals in which the fund buys securities with an agreement that the seller will actually repurchase them within a short time—generally seven days or less—at a price that includes interest for that time. The fund holds the securities as collateral.

Yankee CDs. Certificates issued by U.S. branches of foreign banks.

Safety

How safe are money market funds? Although they are not federally insured, they are considered very safe. Since they began in 1972 two money market funds have failed: First Multifund of New York, which was paying an extremely high rate—93 cents on the dollar—back in 1979.

Recently another fund, Community Bankers U.S. Government

Money Market Fund was forced to liquidate due to risky derivative investments. As we go to press investors are expected to receive 94 cents on their dollar. (See below for a discussion of derivatives.)

The law regulating these funds adds to their safety level: only 5 percent of a fund's assets may be held in obligations of any one institution other than obligations of the U.S. Government. This ruling further adds to the safety of the funds.

Two services provide continually updated professional rankings and safety ratings of the money market mutual funds. Call or write for complimentary copies of the following newsletters:

> "Income & Safety"　　　　　(monthly; $49/year)
> Institute for Econometric Research
> 3471 North Federal Highway
> Fort Lauderdale, FL 33306
> 305-563-9000; 800-327-6720

> "Donoghue's Moneyletter"　　(twice monthly; $127/year)
> 290 Eliot Street
> Ashland, MA 01721
> 508-881-2800

Derivatives

Recently there's been a lot of press and considerable concern over funds' use of derivatives in their portfolio. (Derivatives are securities whose value is "derived from" another asset. For example, an option is a derivative investment that obtains value from the security that can be purchased with the option. Futures are also derivatives because their value depends on the price of other securities. The interest on a bond is a derivative.) Mutual funds, and occasionally money market funds, have seen serious losses due to investments in highly speculative derivatives. To counterbalance any loss of faith, the companies that owned and managed the mutual funds, which included banks, bailed out their money market funds so that losses were not passed on to investors.

In June of 1994 the SEC warned money market funds that they should not use "exotic" derivatives, and in some cases ordered taxable funds to remove specific risky derivatives from their funds. However, the SEC has not prohibited all derivatives, which do vary in risk.

If the fund you invest in, or are considering, appears to be outperforming all others by leaps and bounds, it's possible that they are doing so by using highly speculative investments such as derivatives. First, ask. If you don't get a straight answer, your best bet is to pay attention to the funds' annual reports, proxy statements, etc. Second, pay attention to the news. Derivatives have been getting a lot of attention in the press. They were hot news in 1994; new developments are sure to receive attention in the financial press.

If you are very concerned with safety, select a fund that has a high portion of U.S. Government securities in its portfolio, as well as CDs from well-known domestic banks, and top-rated commercial paper (e.g., IBM, General Electric, Exxon). You can find out what is in the fund by writing or calling the fund and asking for a copy of the prospectus, which lists its investments. Specific investments are usually given in the Q reports.

The safest funds of all, of course, are those that invest *only* in U.S. guaranteed securities. You will certainly sacrifice a point or two in exchange for safety. Among the better known funds that invest exclusively in U.S. guaranteed securities are:

- Capital Preservation Fund
  Benham Group
  800-4-SAFETY

- Merrill Lynch Government Fund
  Merrill Lynch
  800-225-1576

- Fidelity U.S. Government Reserves
  Fidelity Investments
  800-544-8888

- T. Rowe Price U.S. Treasury
  Money Market Fund
  T. Rowe Price
  800-638-5660

- Vanguard Money Market Reserves
  Treasury Portfolio
  The Vanguard Group
  800-662-7447

➤**Hint:** Don't pick a fund just because it has the word "government" in its name. That doesn't guarantee safety! Rather, it means that the odds are that the fund invests primarily in government securities. Unfortunately, however, not all funds are scrupulous about the meaning their name implies.

Another method for ensuring low risk is to select a fund whose holdings mature in less than fifty days. Here's why: if Fund A's capital is invested in longer-term holdings and then interest rates rise significantly, that fund's yield to you will be lower than that of Fund B which has shorter-term issues. That's because Fund B will be able to reinvest in new higher yielding instruments sooner than Fund A. In that event, a large number of fund owners might want to sell their shares in Fund A in order to move into a higher-paying fund. In an extreme case—and it would indeed be extreme—the fund might be forced to sell assets at a loss.

Tax-Exempt Money Funds

The dividends you earn on most funds are fully taxable. Some funds, however, invest solely in tax-exempt securities. Therefore their dividends are not taxed by the IRS, only by the state and local government.

A note of caution: Unless you are in a high tax bracket, it doesn't pay to buy into a tax-exempt fund because they have lower yields than taxable money market funds. (See chart, page 32.)

For the day when your taxable income puts you in a high tax bracket, you will want to consider investing in one of these funds:

- Dreyfus Tax-Exempt Money Market Fund
  800-645-6561
- Franklin Tax-Exempt Money Market Fund
  800-342-5236
- Lexington Tax-Free Money Fund
  800-526-0056

Double and Triple Tax-Exempt Money Funds

If you live in a state with high income tax rates, you can get an even greater tax break from a fund in which interest earned is free of state and federal income taxes, and in many cases, local taxes. A list regularly appears in the *Wall Street Journal* and *Money* magazine. Among the best known are:

- Fidelity *Massachusetts* Tax-Free Money Market
  800-544-8888
- Pru-Bache *New York* Municipal Money Market Fund
  800-222-4321
- Vanguard *California* Tax-Free Money Market Fund
  800-662-7447
- Calvert Tax-Free *California* Portfolio
  800-368-2748
- AIM-C Tax-Exempt of *Connecticut*
  800-572-4462
- Fidelity *Michigan* Tax-Free Money Market
  800-544-8888
- Fidelity *New Jersey* Tax-Free Money Market
  800-544-8888
- Fidelity *Ohio* Tax-Free Money Market
  800-544-8888
- Fidelity *Florida* Tax-Free Money Market
  800-544-8888
- Fidelity *Pennsylvania* Tax-Free Money Market
  800-544-8888
- Dreyfus *New York* Municipal Money Market
  800-645-6561

SHOULD YOU BUY A TAX-EXEMPT FUND?

To determine if a tax-exempt fund is worthwhile:
1) Subtract your tax bracket (28% in this example), from the number 1.
   1 minus .28 = .72
2) Then, divide the tax-free yield the fund is paying by .72 to find the taxable equivalent.
3) The result is the yield you'd need on a taxable investment to match the tax-free yield. For example, if a tax-free investment is yielding 5.5 percent, divide 5.5 by .72. The result, 7.64, is the yield you'd need to beat with a taxable investment if you're in the 28 percent tax bracket.

6

Bank Money Market Deposit Accounts

Top-notch protection *and* liquidity. This almost unbeatable combination is available when you open a **money market deposit account (MMDA)** at your bank. These accounts are insured for up to $100,000 and also pay money market rates without locking up your money for any given period. They are, in fact, an insured variation of the regular money market mutual fund discussed in Chapter 5.

Rules and Regulations

Originally, federal law required a minimum balance of $2,500 to maintain an MMDA. In 1985 the minimum was dropped to $1,000, and today there is no required minimum at all, so banks set their own, with the minimum at $1,000, $1,500, or $2,500.

Keep in mind that both yields and penalties imposed for falling below the minimum vary widely from bank to bank. Once again, it pays to shop around. Use a bank that lets you transfer funds from a MMDA into an ordinary checking account by telephone or ATM (automatic teller machine).

With a bank money market deposit account, you can write only three checks per month (to a third party) against your balance, although you are allowed to withdraw money in person as often as you like—as long as you maintain your minimum balance. Usually there is no minimum amount on the size of the checks.

The interest rate on these accounts is generally, but not always, half a percentage point below that of Treasury bills. Banks adjust the rate periodically along with changes in short-term interest rates. Yields for money market deposit accounts tend to be a little lower than for money market mutual funds. As of October 1994, for example, the national average for money market deposit accounts is 2.56 percent compared to 4.4 percent for money market funds.

There is a key difference in the way in which interest is paid to depositors of money market deposit accounts and to shareholders in a money market mutual fund. Money market mutual funds *must* pay out most of their earnings to the fund's shareholders (only a percentage is retained to cover the cost of operating the fund).

Banks, on the other hand, are not required to pay out all that they earn, but they are obliged by law to post the interest rate they will pay each month. Although banks can pay whatever rate they want, in general you can expect bank rates to be slightly lower than those paid on money market mutual funds, since the money in the bank is insured.

If you're an active investor or a saver who tends to move money around a lot, this multipurpose account could be extremely useful. You get immediate access to your money and it allows you to use other bank services as well.

MUTUAL FUND OR BANK FOR YOUR MONEY MARKET?

Money Market Mutual Fund	Bank Money Market Deposit Account
•Best for those who switch from bonds to stocks to money market funds as interest rates change	•Best for those who want their savings federally insured
•Best for those who plan to write checks against their account	•Best for those who do not need to write more than three checks per month
•You can write as many checks as you like ($150 or $500 minimum per check is common)	•You can write only three checks per month to third parties
	•You can withdraw money in person as often as you like
•No service charges	•Penalties for dropping below minimum balance
•Not insured	•Insured up to $100,000

34

BANK MONEY MARKET DEPOSIT ACCOUNT

For Whom

- Investors who know they can maintain the minimum balance
- Those who want current market rates and instant liquidity
- Those seeking a safe parking place for their savings or emergency money

Minimum

- Determined by individual banks; typically $1,000, $2,000, or $2,500

Safety Factor

- Very high
- Insured up to $100,000

Advantages

- Competitive interest rates
- You can transfer money to checking account (three preauthorized transfers per month)
- You can withdraw money in person as often as you like
- You can get money out easily if interest rates drop

Disadvantages

- Some banks have penalties for withdrawal
- You must maintain a minimum balance, determined by the bank
- You can write only three checks per month
- If balance falls below minimum, interest rate may revert back to passbook rate
- If balance falls below minimum, some banks will pay no interest at all
- If balance falls below minimum, some banks impose a monthly charge and may or may not pay interest

Special Hints

- Find a bank money market deposit account that can be linked electronically to other accounts and to the bank's automatic teller machine network. Then you can write more than the three minimum checks since there is no limit on how often you can personally make transfers. In other words, if the accounts are connected, you can keep most of your money in the higher-paying MMDA and transfer funds into your checking account only as you need to.
- Select a bank that allows you to connect your MMDA to a brokerage account so you can buy stocks, bonds, and Treasuries via telephone.
- Look at the effective annual yield. That is easier to compare than deciphering each different bank's compounding methods.
- Find out if your interest rate will be lowered to passbook rate if your account falls below the required minimum. Find a bank that cuts the rate only for the days when your balance is below the minimum, not one that penalizes you for the entire week or month.

7

Certificates of Deposit

Certificates of deposit, called **CDs,** are time certificates sold by banks. They are issued for a specified amount of money for a specified period. If you are looking for safety and competitive yields, this is the place for you. You agree to leave a certain amount of money with the bank, S&L, or credit union for a stated amount of time, ranging from a few months to several years. When that time period is up, the CD "matures" or "comes due" and you get the full amount plus interest back. And CDs purchased at FDIC-insured institutions are insured for up to $100,000.

Minimum deposits vary from several hundred dollars up to several thousand dollars. Large CDs—those of $100,000 and up—are called **jumbo CDs. They tend to pay slightly higher rates than smaller-sized CDs.**

CDs with a Twist

A number of variations on the traditional CD have emerged in recent years. Below are some examples:

- A comparatively new type of CD, called a "bump-up" CD, allows investors to take advantage of rising interest rates. These CDs allow purchasers to move up to a higher interest rate, usually only once, during the term of the deposit.
- Other new CDs carry built-in rate increases.
- Some CDs, primarily longer-term CDs, now allow investors to withdraw a portion of their funds without penalty within a specified period of time. (Remember, if you take out even a portion of your money, you will adversely effect the yield you expected.)

As always, be sure to ask questions, compare yields—not rates, and read the fine print.

Differences Among Bank CDs

Because banks have various types of CDs, it's essential that you investigate as many as possible when looking for a CD. Don't assume they all have more or less the same rates, because it's just not true. The national average for six month CDs, as of October 1994 was 3.9 percent, but CDs were available for as high as 5.4 to 5.5 percent. Minimums vary. Rates vary. Compounding methods vary. Maturities vary.

In general, you will find that:

- Interest rates on similar CDs offered by different banks in the same city can vary by as much as one full percentage point, or more.
- You will earn more on your CD if the interest is compounded daily.
- Some banks "tier" their interest rates, which means they pay higher interest on larger deposits.
- Banks can set any maturities they wish.
- Some banks will let you set your own maturity date in what are called "designer CDs." If you have to prepare for college tuition, for instance, you can buy a CD that comes due when your child goes off to school in September.

Designer CDs are also ideal for anyone expecting a baby or anticipating retiring at a certain date.

When shopping for a CD, ask your banker about the institution's policy regarding penalties for cashing in a certificate before it matures. CDs of one year or less may carry a penalty of thirty-one days' interest; longer term CDs may carry a penalty of as much as six months' interest. On deposits of one year or more, ninety days' interest is not unusual. Not all banks have the same penalties.

Depending upon where you live, and the number of area banks competing for your money, you will find that CD minimums range from about $500 to $1,000. CDs that remain on deposit for over a year are often available for only $500. Watch for periodic local interest-rate wars and take advantage of temporarily higher rates.

CDs VERSUS OTHER CASH ALTERNATIVES

Vs. Money Markets

Although CDs of one year or less tend to pay slightly higher rates than bank money market accounts, you give up immediate access to your money.

Vs. Treasury Notes

Before you buy a longer-term CD, compare the rate to a Treasury note. (See pages 87–95.) An advantage T-notes offer is that their interest is free from state and local taxes.

Buying a CD from Your Broker

In addition to being able to buy CDs at your bank, you can also buy them through a stockbroker. The advantage is you escape those hefty early-withdrawal penalties the banks impose, since you can sell your bank CD to the brokerage firm. And, you will get the same yields as well as FDIC insurance.

Here's how it works. *First,* you tell your broker what CD maturity you want. He will quote a rate. Since the bank pays the broker to sell the CD, you will not be stuck paying your broker a commission. Then you proceed to buy the CD.

Second, if you want to redeem it before maturity, you can sell it back to the broker without a penalty—he can readily sell it to someone else in the "secondary market."

🛑 *Caution:* The price of the CD will fluctuate depending upon what it's worth on the open market. To be more specific, your CD will go up in price if interest rates go down—that's because it is more prized by investors than newly issued CDs which have lower rates. On the other hand, it will decrease in value if money market interest rates rise. That means it is sometimes possible to make a profit by actually cashing in a CD early.

STOP *Caution:* Savers who bought CDs of weak banks through brokers will have to move them when they mature. Under new FDIC rules that took effect in June 1992, banks that do not meet minimum capital requirements will not be able to accept brokered CDs. Current CDs will be grandfathered, but they cannot be renewed or rolled over.

The FDIC says about 570 banks are undercapitalized although it's not making the list public.

CHECKLIST

- Call two or three banks as well as your broker to see who has the highest rate.
- Ask how the interest is calculated. Daily, remember, is better than weekly or quarterly.
- You may get a slightly higher rate at your broker's office because he buys huge certificates of $100,000 or more and then sells you a $1,000 chunk. These jumbo certificates pay higher interest rates than the smaller bank CDs. You may also get a higher rate than at your local banks because brokerage firms shop the nation for the highest yielding CDs.
- Make certain that the brokerage house will keep track of your CDs and mail you the interest if you like, or reinvest it if that is your wish.
- Find out the rating (the financial standing) of the bank issuing the CD. Merrill Lynch, for example, provides credit ratings on its CDs.

Choosing a CD Interest Rate

Advertising by financial institutions may herald high rates in order to entice you and your money. But before you buy a certificate of deposit from a bank, read the fine print and figure out the interest rate.

- *Compounding*. Note whether the ad says interest is compounded or simple. Compounded is better because it means your interest earns interest. If compounded, is it done annually, semiannually, monthly, daily? It makes a difference. On a one-year certificate of deposit that pays 5 percent simple, interest is just that—5 percent. But when compounded daily, that 5 percent yields the equivalent of 5.33 percent over the course of a year.
- *Floating Rates*. Some accounts and CDs have floating rates in which interest is tied to an index, such as rates on U.S. Treasury securities. Banks should explain the initial rate, and most do, but they cannot tell you what the long-term rate will be, since it fluctuates.
- *Teaser Rates*. Some institutions offer a high introductory rate, which then drops. The high rate is apt to appear in the ads, the low rate in the fine print.
- *Annual Yields*. Often the yield given in an ad is for one year or less, and it assumes upon maturity (all interest rates are quoted on an annual basis) that you will reinvest all the money in another CD paying the same rate. In other words, if you don't roll over your CD, or if you roll it over into an account paying a lower rate, you won't get the advertised yield.
- *To Protect Yourself*. Ask your banker:

  1) What the interest rate will be during the entire life of a fixed rate CD
  2) What the effective annual yield is
  3) What the penalties are for early withdrawal

  4) *Highest Yields*. Check the Wednesday edition of the *Wall Street Journal* for listings of the nation's highest-yielding CDs. If rates are significantly higher out-of-town, call for instructions on purchasing them. Other newspapers and magazines publish similar lists.

8

Mini-Investor Programs

Once you have tucked away a small nest egg, then $500, believe it or not, can move you into the stock market. There are several interesting programs especially designed for the mini-investor; but remember, stocks are more risky than any of the previously mentioned vehicles.

🛑 *Caution:* These mini-programs are not designed to take the place of a savings account. They are merely an inexpensive way to buy stocks because they side-step buying and selling stocks through a broker, thus eliminating the expensive commissions brokerage firms charge for small trades. For example, 100 shares of a $50 stock will cost between $97 and $108 in brokerage commissions from "full-service" firms like Merrill Lynch, PaineWebber, and others. A discount firm, on the other hand, charges around $49 for the same purchase. (Suggestions for what stocks to buy can be found in Chapter 17.)

🛑 *Caution:* Participation is suggested only after you have saved at least three months living expenses for an emergency.

What Is a Stock?

Before becoming involved in the stock market, it's important that you understand what a stock is. A stock represents part ownership in a company, and anyone who owns a stock is called a stockholder or shareholder. When a company wants to raise capital to expand, it can borrow money from the bank or it can issue, or sell, stocks and bonds to the public. (See Chapter 16 on bonds and Chapter 17 for more on stocks.)

In order to document the fact that people purchase stock, the company issues a stock certificate to each shareholder. This piece of paper shows the number of shares owned by that person.

If the company is profitable, the owners of common stock share in the profits in two ways: They gain income through **dividends** and dividend increases, and they benefit as the stock increases in price, known as **appreciation**. A dividend is a periodic cash payment made from a company's earnings to stockholders. Most dividends are paid four times a year. The board of directors can increase, decrease, or even cancel dividends, depending upon the company's profits. Dividend payments vary from stock to stock. In fact, some companies never pay dividends. Those that consistently pay dividends are known as **income stocks** and investors buy them precisely because they want the steady cash payments. Utility stocks, which are one of the best and largest categories of income stocks, are discussed in Chapter 12. The stocks of companies that pay little or no dividends are known as **growth stocks**. Investors buy them because they expect the price of the stock to grow over time. Growth stocks, which are riskier than income stocks, are discussed in Chapter 17.

You may buy stocks in any publicly held corporation—one whose shares are traded publicly. (Many U.S. companies are privately held and do not sell shares to the public.) In addition to individuals, institutions also buy stocks. **Institutional investors** include employee pension funds and mutual funds.

Stocks are sold to the public in two steps: Initially they are sold in the **primary market**; thereafter, these same stocks are resold to other investors through a stock exchange in what is called the **secondary market**. The secondary market is not any one place but includes the New York, American, and regional stock exchanges as well as the over-the-counter market. These exchanges are marketplaces where certain qualified stocks approved by the exchange are listed for buying and selling. The exchanges do not own the stocks nor do they influence the price. They merely function as an auction place. Although the price of a stock is fixed when it is initially offered for sale to the public, its price continually fluctuates thereafter, depending upon the interest of buyers and sellers at the time.

Here are four ways you can get into the action with your $500 and at a reasonable rate.

Buying Stock Directly

You can bypass stockbrokers altogether by going directly to the company to buy its stock. Only a handful of public companies offer this unique service, but you can expect more to join the bandwagon. Contact the Shareholder Relations Division at:

- Central Vermont Public Service
  Rutland, VT
  802-773-2711
- Exxon
  New York, NY
  c/o First Chicago
  800-252-1800

- Interchange Financial Services
  Saddle Brook, NJ
  201-703-2265
- Johnson Controls, Inc.
  Milwaukee, WI
  414-228-1200
- Texaco
  White Plains, NY
  914-253-4000

The following companies allow first-time purchases for customers and/or residents of the state in which the company operates.

- American Recreation Centers, Inc.
  Rancho Cordova, CA
  916-852-8005
- Bancorp Hawaii
  Honolulu, Hawaii
  808-537-8239
- Barnett Banks of Florida
  Jacksonville, FL
  904-791-7500 or 800-524-4458

You can purchase stock directly from these public utility companies if you live in an area serviced by them:

Carolina Power & Light
Central Hudson Gas & Electric
Central Main Power
Cleveland Electric Illuminating
Dominion Resources
Duke Power
Hawaiian Electric Industries
Idaho Power
Minnesota Power & Light
Montana Power
National Fuel & Gas (NY & PA)
Nevada Power
Philadelphia Suburban
Portland General Electric
Puget Sound Power & Light
San Diego Gas & Electric
Southwest Gas (Nevada)
Union Electric (Missouri)
Wisconsin Energy

➤ **Hint:** To find out if you can purchase stock from any publicly traded company directly, write or call the Shareholder Relations Department.

Dividend Reinvestment Plans

It Pays To Be a DRIP

No one likes to pay brokerage commissions, even to a friendly broker. In fact, they prevent some small investors from buying stocks at all. Here's another way around this dilemma: Over a thousand companies permit existing shareholders to participate in a DRIP (Dividend Reinvestment Program). These plans allow investors who already own stock in a company to buy additional shares by automatically reinvesting their dividends. Many are solid blue chip companies (such as AT&T, Clorox, Du Pont, Heinz, Texaco, Procter & Gamble, and Kellogg) or public utilities that pay above-average dividends. Although some companies do charge a nominal fee, none charge what a broker would. Many also offer 3 to 5 percent off the market price of new shares, so you're really paying a lower price than you would through a stockbroker. Quite a few also allow shareholders to make cash payments into the plan to accumulate more shares in their accounts. For example, AT&T has an optional cash plan of $25 or more up to a maximum of $7,500 monthly. Dividend reinvestment is done entirely through the company—no broker is involved.

➤**Hint:** If you already own stock in a company, call the Shareholder Relations Division and ask if the company has a DRIP and, if so, how many shares you need to enroll. With some companies, a single share is sufficient; others require 15, 50, or 100 shares.

SELECTED STOCKS WITH
REINVESTMENT PLANS

Plans with No Discount

American Home Products	IBM
Atlanta Gas & Light	Kimberly-Clark
BellSouth	NYNEX
Consolidated Edison	Tambrands
Exxon	TECO Energy
Ford	Travelers
General Motors	U.S. West
Harland (John H.)	Wisconsin Energy

Plans With a 5 Percent Discount

Citizens & Southern	Security Pacific
Fleet/Norstar	Signet Banking
MNC Financial	Southeast Banking

Plans With a 3 Percent Discount

Bank of Boston	J.P. Morgan
Citicorp	

➤**Hint:** For a complete listing of companies with DRIPS, contact Dow Theory Forecasts, Inc., 7412 Calumet Ave., Hammond, IN 43624-2692; 219-931-6480; cost: $15.95 including shipping.

Two More Low-Cost Ways To Buy Stocks

- *Buying One Share.* Individual investors may join the National Association of Investment Clubs. (NAIC's address and more information are found in Chapter 9.) Under NAIC's "Low-Cost Investment Plan" for a one-time charge of $5 per company, you can buy as little as one share directly from more than 120 major participating corporations, including Whirlpool, Kellogg, McDonald's, Mobil, and Quaker Oats. Most do not charge a commission, although a few require a nominal fee ($1 to $3) for each transaction to cover expenses. All have Dividend Reinvestment Programs.

- *Buying at Work.* An increasing number of companies offer plans through which employees can buy stock in their company called ESOPs, or Employee Stock Ownership Plans. Check with your benefits officer to see if your employer offers this option. According to the Employees Benefit Research Institute, the most popular plan is one that permits employees to contribute up to 6 percent of their salary and then the firm matches half that contribution.

The Blueprint Program™

An inexpensive and convenient way for you to invest in stocks has been devised by Merrill Lynch, the nation's largest full-service brokerage firm. Through the Blueprint Program™, you can now invest any dollar amount you want, the initial minimum being $500. The interesting aspect of this program is that you're investing by the dollar amount, not by the share, which means you can acquire fractions of shares as well as whole shares. You may buy any stock that trades on the New York and American Stock Exchanges and many over-the-counter stocks. Merrill Lynch's list of recommended stocks for participants in the Blueprint Program™, updated periodically, will be sent to participants upon request. It consists of stocks with above-average dividend yields or long-term growth potential. Blueprint Program™ participants get a break on commissions. The firm charges up to 55 percent less than regular Merrill Lynch fees on stock transactions.

BLUEPRINT PROGRAM™

For Whom

- Any small investor interested in getting into the market with minimal expenditures

Where to Purchase

- Your local Merrill Lynch office, or from:

The Blueprint Program
Box 30441
New Brunswick, NJ 08989-0441
800-637-3766

Minimum and Fees

- $500
- Commission is discounted up to 55 percent from regular fees

Safety Factor

- Like any stock purchase, safety depends on the price changes in the stock

Advantages

- Low entry cost
- Merrill Lynch research and professional assistance
- Diversification
- Liquidity
- Reduced brokerage fees
- Optional automatic dividend reinvestment plan
- Company annual report will be sent to you as soon as you have one full share of any security

- Record keeping and tax data are taken care of by Merrill Lynch
- Dollar cost averaging

Disadvantages

- Risk is equal to that of the stock market

DOLLAR COST AVERAGING

While no investment plan is risk-free, dollar cost averaging, a technique offered by the Blueprint Program, can help cushion you from stock market fluctuations. With dollar cost averaging you invest the same fixed dollar amount every month in the same stock—say $25, $50 or $100. That means you buy more shares when prices go down and fewer when prices go up. Over the long run, you get a lower average cost per unit for the investments you make. *Note:* You can cancel this plan at any time. You can also use dollar cost averaging on your own or with mutual funds.

9

Investment Clubs

Of all the options you have at your doorstep, a clubhouse will provide you with the most fun and enjoyment—if not the greatest return on your principal—as a home for your small investment.

Joining an investment club is an excellent way to learn about the stock market, the movement of interest rates, and the overall economy. It is also a means of meeting new people who, like you, are interested in learning how to turn a small amount of money into a sizeable investment.

Most clubs are small—optimum size is about twenty—and they meet once or twice a month in a community center or in a member's home. Members pool their money and jointly purchase shares of stock. Clubs require monthly payments that can range from $20 per month to as high as the members dare go. Energetic hosts frequently combine the regular business meeting and discussion with coffee, dessert, or other refreshments.

The mechanics are simple. Making money, though, is not—especially if most members are inexperienced. Nevertheless, you will get your investment feet wet, and by combining your collective dollars and knowledge, you'll undoubtedly pick a winner or two!

If you don't know of a club in your area, ask at work or at a local YMCA or YWCA, adult education center, church, or synagogue. If you cannot find a club to join, start your own with a few friends or colleagues. The steps are easy:

1) Find twelve to twenty people willing to join a club. Set the minimum investment requirement ahead of time—the average is $40/month.
2) Select a person to be responsible for paper work. This task should rotate every few months.
3) For details on how to get started, contact the National

Association of Investment Clubs, 711 West 13 Mile Rd., Madison Heights, MI 48071, 810-583-6242, the umbrella group for all clubs. Your club may join this association for $35, plus $11 per member. You will receive a stack of useful literature plus a subscription to *Better Investing* magazine. The NAIC also gives member clubs extremely useful and solid advice on the legal aspects of organizing a club, conducting meetings, analyzing stocks, and setting up portfolios. (Individuals can join NAIC for $35.)

4) Establish firm guidelines regarding withdrawal of a member's funds and entry of new members.

5) Meet and invest on a regular basis—whether or not the market is doing well.

6) Reinvest all earnings in a diversified portfolio—one that has at least five different companies.

7) Use a discount broker to save on commission fees.

8) Stick to regular stock buy-and-sell guidelines. All members should be responsible, on a regular, rotating basis, for doing research and making recommendations to the club.

Do Clubs Really Make Money?

Yes, many of them do. According to a recent NAIC survey, twenty-six out of the last thirty-eight years, clubs bettered the S&P 500's total return. The secret to their success is that member clubs follow a program of patient, long-term investing. They adhere to these principles:

- Invest a fixed monthly amount, without regard to the stock market outlook. Clubs that try to outguess the market usually fail.
- Reinvest all earnings to achieve the advantage of compound income.
- Invest in solid growth companies whose sales and earnings are increasing faster than the economy or those of competing firms.
- Diversify investments to spread out risk.

INVESTMENT CLUBS

For Whom

- Anyone

Minimum

- Set by individual clubs. Ranges from $20 per month up. Members contribute a set amount on a monthly basis.

Safety Factor

- Depends on the club's investment philosophy

Advantages

- Inexpensive and supportive way to learn about investing
- Reduces anxiety surrounding first-time investing and trading
- Individual members of the NAIC can buy one share of any of a number of companies and thereafter invest small amounts periodically in these companies (See Chapter 8)

Disadvantages

- You may earn a better return elsewhere, especially if your club is inexperienced or does not set sensible buy and sell guidelines
- Results are not guaranteed
- Investment is not insured
- High mortality rate—many clubs fail in the first twelve to eighteen months

HOW YOUR $50 WILL GROW

	One Year	Five Years	Ten Years
Bank Coupon Club (2% compounded daily)	$51.01	$55.27	$61.12
Bank Savings Account (3% compounded daily)	51.52	58.09	67.49
EE Savings Bond (4% compounded daily)	52.04	61.07	74.59
Money Market Fund (5% compounded daily)	52.56	64.20	82.87
Money Market Fund (6% compounded daily)	53.09	67.49	91.10

HOW MONTHLY SAVINGS ADD UP

Look at what happens if you invest $100, $300, or $500 each month at a fixed rate of 8%, not taking taxes into consideration.

Monthly Amount	Number of Years		
	5	10	20
$100	$ 7,348	$18,295	$ 58,902
$300	22,043	54,884	176,706
$500	36,738	91,473	294,510

Source: Credit Union National Association, Inc.

PART THREE

The First $1,000

10

Your IRA, Keogh, or SEP

Without a doubt, the very first $1,000 that you manage to accumulate should be invested in an **IRA** (individual retirement account), in a **Keogh plan,** or a **Simplified Employee Pension Plan,** also known as a **SEP.**

An IRA, just as its name implies, is a tax-advantaged account into which individuals contribute money that is invested for their retirement.

A Keogh plan is a similar tax-advantaged account designed for those who are self-employed. The money invested in both grows free of taxes until it is taken out. That means interest and dividend income accumulates on a tax-deferred basis.

A SEP, also for the self-employed, is best for small businesses and sole proprietors. It's considerably easier to set up and administer than a Keogh.

Life expectancy for an American baby born today is well over 70 years. That means most of us will eventually spend a number of years in retirement, so it goes without saying that preparing for the time when we're not working has become an absolute necessity unless we want to face melted cheese and tuna casseroles for dinner day in and day out during our golden years.

The recent turmoil over the financial well-being of the Social Security system has, or should have, alerted everyone to the fact that it can no longer be counted on as basic income for retirement. Even government-supported medical benefits have been tightened, reducing the portion of a retiree's bill covered by the system. You should regard Social Security only as a means for covering subsistence-level items. At most, Social Security benefits replace only 24% of salary for someone earning $60,000 upon retirement and 43% of salary for someone earning $24,090.

Companies are getting wise, too, and are not always inclined to be any more generous than they have to be. Pension plans have been trending downward and benefits are generally being reduced.

Bailouts have been necessary to rescue the Social Security system, railroad, and other large federal retirement systems. And other private retirement systems consistently come under the gun as programs teeter under the weight of huge payments to beneficiaries. Keep in mind, too, that more and more companies are tapping pension coffers to raise dollars for expansion, mergers, etc. During the past several years, over 135 companies actually closed out their retirement plans. Many substituted less expensive programs.

So, it makes sense that every American should have an IRA, Keogh, SEP, or **401(k) plan,** or as many as possible. A 401(k) plan is one in which your company deducts a certain amount from your salary upon your request and puts it into a retirement account. It is also known as a salary-reduction plan. (See Chapter 11.)

➤**Hint:** According to investment advisors Scudder, Stevens and Clark, if at age 25 you start to save $2,000 a year in an IRA yielding only 5 percent a year, you will accumulate $242,000 by age 65. At an annual rate of 10 percent, that amount would grow to $885,000. So fund your IRA starting today!

WHAT YOU WILL HAVE WHEN YOU ARE 65

Age when start saving $2,000 per year in an IRA	Annual rate of return		
	5%	10%	15%
25	$242,000	$885,000	$3,558,000
35	133,000	329,000	869,000
45	66,000	115,000	205,000
55	25,000	32,000	41,000

How Does an IRA Work?

- Anyone who is working can put up to 100 percent of the first $2,000 he or she earns annually into an IRA every year. If you earn less than $2,000 a year—let's say $1,275— you could contribute that entire amount. But even if you're a rock star making millions of dollars every year, $2,000 is still the maximum you can contribute annually.

- Although there is a maximum yearly contribution of $2,000, your IRA will increase in value just through the interest earned or the dividends paid out. These additional dollars stay in the account along with whatever you contribute, until you retire and begin withdrawing your money. If like most retirees, you're in a lower tax bracket when you're retired, there will be less of a tax bite when you do start tapping your account.

- If both husband and wife work, each can contribute $2,000 to separate accounts every year and take $4,000 off their joint income tax return. If one spouse does not work, then the working spouse can contribute up to $2,250 to a "spousal account." *Note:* In a spousal account, some portion of the money must be set aside in each spouse's name; it need not be equal amounts.

- If you are divorced and receive alimony, you can make an IRA contribution even if all your income is from alimony, as it is treated as earned income.
- Your contribution is tax deductible provided neither you nor your spouse is an active participant in an employer-sponsored retirement plan and you are younger than age 70-1/2 at the end of the year.
- Even if you or your spouse is an active participant in a plan, you may still be able to deduct IRA contributions on a sliding scale; check with your accountant. The deduction is eliminated when adjusted gross income reaches $50,000 for a married couple or $35,000 for an unmarried person.
- Even if you are no longer eligible for the $2,000 deduction, do not abandon your IRA. It is still an excellent way to accumulate tax-deferred earnings for the day when you retire.
- You may have use of your IRA dollars once a year for a sixty-day period through a procedure called a **rollover** in which you actually take money out of one IRA account and put it into another one. But beware: Unless your assets are in another IRA within sixty days, you will have to pay both income tax and the added 10 percent penalty tax. Some people find a rollover useful if they need cash for less than sixty days.

What the Numbers Show

Investment performance in an IRA far outstrips similar investments made in the taxable world. The table below shows the benefits of putting $2,000 a year in an IRA that compounds at 8 percent compared to putting the same amount in a taxable investment, assuming you're in the 28 percent tax bracket.

IRA VS. TAXABLE INVESTMENT		
Years	IRA Account	Taxable Account
5	$11,924	$11,867
10	28,130	27,568
15	50,627	48,343
20	82,369	75,831

Where to Invest Your IRA, Keogh, or SEP

Whether you're inclined to be conservative or speculative, there's an investment program that's just right for your IRA, Keogh, or SEP. Several **custodians** are officially approved as places to set up IRAs—banks, brokerage firms, and mutual funds are the most popular. Consider all three before opening your account, taking into consideration how much money you have, your interest in monitoring your account, and your appetite for risk. You'll also want to compare custodial charges which generally run from $10 to $50 and closing fees which are sometimes even higher.

➤**Hint:** Be sure to pay the custodial fee with a separate check so it won't reduce your account, and get it in the mail by December 31 so you can deduct it on your tax return if your miscellaneous expenses exceed 2 percent of your adjusted gross income.

Deciding where to put your IRA and Keogh dollars is very much related to personal temperament as well as market timing. If you tend to be cautious, or if you're nervous watching the stock market go up and down, then simply begin with a bank CD. Since CD rates are low but rising as we go to press, you should not tie up all your money long-term in a CD. Select a CD that matures in a year or less so if rates continue to rise you can re-invest it and get a better return. If you enjoy playing the market and are astute in selecting top quality stocks and bonds, consider putting your plan with a broker. If you want professional management, then use a mutual fund.

Here is a thumbnail sketch of your custodian choices. Remember that although you can divide your IRA contributions into as many investment choices and custodians as you like (as long as you stay within the dollar limitations), it's best to limit those choices to a reasonable number. It's difficult to keep track of too many plans and to continually make that many investment decisions. Most plans require a lower minimum than for regular accounts, with $250 being fairly typical.

The IRS lets you fund IRAs with stocks, bonds, mutual funds, government and agency issues, CDs, foreign securities, covered options, and financial and commodity futures. It does not allow investments bought on margin, insurance investments, and collectible objects, except U.S. and state gold and silver coins of one ounce or less.

Banks

The safest and probably the most convenient choice for a small IRA is a bank **CD** or certificate of deposit which is insured up to $100,000. Most banks, savings and loans, and credit unions charge little or nothing to set up and maintain an IRA. Some, however, impose monthly maintenance charges. That means, as in every institutional transaction, you absolutely must read the fine print carefully.

Bank CDs pay whatever rate of interest the bank wants, and these rates vary considerably among individual institutions. Most have fixed interest rates, while some have variable rates that float up and down with general interest rates. Bank CDs range in length from several months to several years. Think carefully before deciding how long a term CD to buy.

🛑 *Caution:* There's a risk involved in buying a long-term CD, say one that matures or comes due in five years, because rates may go up during that five-year period, thus making your original investment, with its locked-in interest rate, less attractive than newer, higher-yielding CDs. The shorter the CD's time period, the more conservative your play. It is true you are at a disadvantage if rates fall, but if you lock in a long-term rate, you eliminate the chance of taking advantage of rising interest rates.

Mutual Funds

The inner workings of **mutual funds** are explained in great detail in Chapters 5 and 13. But as far as the pros and cons of using one for your IRA or Keogh plan are concerned, here is what you should know.

Just about all mutual funds—which are companies that pool money together from individuals in order to buy a wide variety of stocks, bonds, and Treasuries—offer IRAs. Even though you can find a mutual fund specializing in gold, commodities, or foreign stocks, your own good judgment should steer you in more sane directions. Remember—you're saving for your own retirement.

Instead, select mutual funds that invest in money market funds, high quality common stocks selected for appreciation or dividend income, and top rated bonds.

🛑 *Caution:* Steer clear of funds that are already tax exempt. Since IRAs are sheltered from taxes, you don't need that feature. Tax-exempt funds pay slightly lower returns than taxable funds.

How do mutual funds compare with bank CDs for your IRA or Keogh?

Brokerage Firms

At some point down the road, when you feel confident about picking stocks and bonds and you have close to $5,000 in your IRA account, consider opening a "self-directed" IRA through a brokerage firm. You will manage the funds, but the broker will serve as custodian, collecting the commission on your buy and sell trades. He can also advise you on what stocks and bonds to include in your IRA.

When your IRA is small, this type of account hardly pays since you don't have enough money with which to diversify. In other words, the amount is not sufficient to spread out over several different stocks or bonds. And, on top of that, the brokerage fees are high in relation to the size of your account. (See page 62 for a sample of commission fees.) If eventually, however, you decide to run your own IRA, try doing it through a discount broker where the fees are substantially lower.

A MUTUAL FUND FOR YOUR IRA?

Pros
- Potential for substantial gains
- For those prepared to take some risk
- For those who don't want to pick their own stocks or bonds
- Over the long term, stocks tend to outpace other investments
- A professional is managing your money
- Easy to neglect monitoring your fund's performance
- Dividends or earnings can be automatically reinvested in additional shares
- Better returns may be available elsewhere

Cons
- Not insured
- Vulnerable to market risks
- Changes in value with the stock market or interest rates
- A fee is charged for setting up an IRA
- There will be sales fees when buying and selling shares unless you select a no-load fund

COMPARE BROKERAGE COMMISSIONS

	100 shares @ $40	100 shares @ $30	100 shares @ $20
Quick & Reilly	$49	$82	$109
Charles Schwab	55	107	144
Fidelity	54	106	144
Merrill Lynch	100	204	374

Suggested Stocks for an IRA

These conservative stocks are suggested for long-term total return:

ALLTELL Corp

American Home Products

Atlanta Gas Light

Brooklyn Union Gas

Kellogg

Mobil Corp.

Procter & Gamble

Potomac Electric Power

Southwestern Bell

TECO Energy

Whirlpool

Wisconsin Energy

Disadvantages of an IRA

- IRAs are not liquid. Although you can withdraw money, the penalties for doing so are stiff.
- IRAs may not be used as collateral.

One of the most helpful booklets on IRAs is free. Contact your nearest Internal Revenue Service for a copy of publication #590, *Individual Retirement Arrangements (IRAs)*, or call 800-829-3676.

Keoghs and SEPs

Keogh Plans

If you are self-employed, either part-time or full-time you should take advantage of the tax benefits offered by a Keogh plan. Anyone who earns income from his or her own business, profession, or skill is entitled to participate in a Keogh as well as in an IRA.

Note: Even if you have an IRA or a private pension plan set up in which to save salaried income, you may still have a Keogh plan in order to shelter that portion of your income that comes from being self-employed.

As with an IRA, you have a number of custodian choices: banks, savings and loans, brokerage houses, mutual funds, and insurance companies. Your contributions are deductible from your federal income tax, and the interest in your account accumulates free of taxes. The same early withdrawal penalties that apply to an IRA apply to a Keogh.

Here's where the two plans differ: In a Keogh you may contribute up to 25 percent of what you earn through self-employment—before tax deductions—for a total of $30,000 annually. If you have high self-employed income, that's a much better deal than the $2,000 IRA maximum. On the other hand, if you're self-employed part-time, the 25 percent ceiling may be rather low.

SEPs

When an employer, which can be you as the sole proprietor, establishes a SEP, the employee then simply opens a SEP IRA. (See choices for an IRA above.) In other words, a SEP is effectively an employer-sponsored IRA. Individual accounts are established for each employee with contributions limited to 13.043 percent of earnings or $30,000, whichever is less. Certain SEPs can include a salary-reduction feature as with a 401(k) plan.

ADVANTAGES OF AN IRA

- Every dollar you contribute can be written off your tax return if you are not a part of a qualified pension fund or if your income is below $25,000 (single) or $40,000 (married).
- If you or your spouse participate in a qualified retirement plan, you may be able to deduct some or all of your contributions depending upon your adjusted gross income (AGI). If you are single, head of household or married filing separately and your AGI is $25,000 or less, you can fully deduct your contribution; if your AGI is above $25,000 but less than $35,000, you can deduct part of it. On joint returns the range is $40,000 to $50,000.
- Penalties discourage IRA withdrawals prior to retirement and thus encourage saving.
- Interest and dividends earned are tax free until withdrawn.

11

Your 401(k) Plan

I've got all the money I'll ever need if I die by four o'clock.
—Henny Youngman

One relatively painless way to make certain you have money to get you past four o'clock as well as through retirement is the 401(k) plan. Offered by many employers to employees, this savings plan has become increasingly popular since it was authorized by Congress in the early 1980s. Since 1988 the share of private companies with 401(k) plans has increased from 10% to 37%. Not only does it provide employees with an automatic way to save for retirement, it also reduces and defers taxes.

With this type of retirement savings plan, also known as a **salary-reduction plan,** you contribute a certain amount of your annual salary to a special retirement account that has been set up by your employer with an authorized institution. The contribution is deducted from your paycheck, so you don't even miss the money. The amount deducted is listed separately on your W-2 form, but is not included in the amount listed for "wages, tips, other compensation." In other words, your contributions are made with pre-tax dollars. Your contribution reduces your reportable salary, which in turn reduces your federal income tax liability.

Many have an added plus: the employer also contributes, in some cases matching dollar for dollar or 50 cents for each dollar the employee pays in.

Most plans let employees decide where to invest their contributions. The typical choices are the company's stock, a stock mutual fund, a long-term bond fund, a money market fund, and a guaranteed investment contract. (GICs are fixed-income investments sponsored by insurance companies with payment of interest and return of principal guaranteed by the insurer but not by the federal government.) Generally, you can move your money among the different investments at least once a year.

Although taxes are postponed until you start receiving the money, there is a 10 percent penalty tax for withdrawing money before age 59-1/2. You must start distributions by age 70-1/2.

➤ **Hint:** Even if you are eligible for a tax deduction on your IRA, contribute to a 401(k), too, if it's offered where you work. The maximum you can put into an IRA is only $2,000 a year, whereas the ceiling on a 401(k) is much higher and indexed for inflation: The 1994 ceiling was $9,240.

Each company that offers employees these plans has its own special designs. Ask your employee benefits officer to explain yours. Many companies match all or part of their employees' contributions.

Withdrawing and Borrowing

You can withdraw funds before age 59-1/2 only if you're facing a financial hardship—for example, if you need to pay funeral or medical expenses for a member of the family or, in some cases, to pay for a principal residence or avoid eviction. The regulations are very stringent. To be eligible for a hardship withdrawal, you must prove that you can't meet your needs by borrowing from a bank or tapping other savings. However, many plans do permit borrowing. Rules on borrowing vary widely from plan to plan. Ask what the interest rate on loans is and how long you have to pay it back.

Many plans now let participants borrow funds—up to half the amount but not more than $50,000. You pay interest on the loan to your own account, typically a percentage point less than what banks charge on secured personal loans. By law, 50 percent of your balance has to stay in the account as security for the loan. The loan must be repaid at least quarterly and fully within five years unless the money goes toward purchase of a principal residence.

➤ **Hint:** The interest rate is often lower than what a bank will charge and, of course, your interest payments accumulate to your account and not to a bank.

12

Public Utilities

What Is a Stock?

A stock, as you recall from Chapter 8, represents part ownership in a company, and anyone who owns a stock is called a stockholder or shareholder.

Stocks of public utility companies have traditionally been sound, high-yielding investments and as such are considered safe enough for "widows and orphans." Because of their generally solid dividends and high safety ranking, you can invest at the $1,000 level, even though other individual common stocks are better purchased with investments of $5,000 or more, or through a mutual fund. In general, of course, the greater the risk element in an investment, the more money you should have to cushion any losses.

And utilities are also appealing because of their dividend reinvestment plans (see Chapter 8). Some utilities even offer a discount when their shares are bought through these plans.

Gas, light, and water companies are rarely subject to competition; in fact, they are usually monopolies. Even in a recession, everybody needs and uses the services they provide, which is why they should be part of every investor's portfolio.

How to Find Bright Lights

Begin in your own backyard:

Step 1

Call the investor or public relations department of your nearest utility company for a copy of the annual report. Take a look through it to see whether:

- Earnings per share are rising
- Dividends are increasing
- Plant construction is completed
- The area's population is growing
- The company is facing any lawsuits

Step 2

Track the company's stock price for several weeks by looking in the newspaper; be alert to trends up or down. Avoid buying shares at their 52-week high. (See pages 118–119 for how to read stock market tables.)

Step 3

Call a local stockbroker for an investment opinion and research report. You can do this whether or not you have an account.

Step 4

Compare the brokerage firm's report with that in *Value Line Investment Survey* or Standard & Poor's *Stock Reports*. These two key reference tools are available at most public libraries and brokerage offices.

Value Line ranks stocks for safety; stick with those with a #1 or #2 ranking.

Step 5

Read any press coverage of the company's prospects or problems.

Step 6

If you decide to buy shares, do so through a discount broker to save on commissions and sign up for the company's dividend reinvestment plan, (DRIP) if it has one.

SIX HIGH YIELDING UTILITY STOCKS

- Orange & Rockland   7.5%
- Allegheny Power   7.4
- Union Electric   7.1
- Carolina Power & Light   6.1
- Brooklyn Union Gas   5.9
- FPL Group   5.4

Rated A by *Standard & Poor's*; yields as of November 1994

PART FOUR

The First $2,000

13

Mutual Funds for Stocks & Ginnie Maes

A mutual fund is a company that makes investments for individuals and institutions. When you buy into a mutual fund you are actually purchasing shares of an investment trust or corporation. Your dollars are pooled with those of hundreds of other investors, and these combined monies are then invested and managed by professionals in large, diversified portfolios of stocks, bonds, and various money market papers. This diversification helps insulate you against wide fluctuations in the prices of individual stocks.

Mutual funds are **open-ended**—that is, like stocks, shares are continually available and they can be bought or sold at any time. Unlike a traditional corporation, mutual funds can issue an unlimited number of shares. The actual price of a fund's share, or its net asset value, is determined at the end of each business day when the fund adds up the value of securities held in its portfolio, subtracts expenses, and divides the total by the number of shares outstanding.

Mutual funds make money for shareholders in three ways: 1) They pay them dividends and interest earned from the fund's investments. 2) If a security (stock or bond) is sold at a profit, the fund pays shareholders *capital gain distributions*. 3) If the value of the securities held by the fund increases, the value of each mutual fund share increases proportionately. Shareholders can have dividends and capital gains reinvested in additional shares of the fund or have the fund send them a check for the earnings.

Choosing a Mutual Fund

Before beginning your search for the right fund, you should know the difference between load and no-load funds.

Load funds, sold by stock brokers and mutual fund salespeople, are "loaded" with a sales charge or fee. Commissions for the purchase or sale of the fund generally range from about 4 percent to 8-1/2 percent of the total price. Keep in mind that this means the value of the fund must escalate by that amount before you can break even. Since studies show there is no evidence that load funds outperform no-loads, you might as well find one without a commission and save the difference for investing. But sometimes people like to buy load funds because they come recommended by their stockbrokers; they find it easier to let the brokers do the fund selection for them.

No-load funds have no sales commissions; you purchase shares directly from the fund itself, not through a stockbroker. But some have hidden fees (see box, page 74). For a complete list of no-load funds, consult:

> *Directory of Mutual Funds* ($8.50)
> Investment Company Institute
> 1401 M Street NW
> Washington, DC 20036

This annual guide lists nearly 500 low-load and no-load mutual funds under 22 different investment objective categories.

The Individual Investor's Guide to Low-Load Mutual Funds ($24.95)
American Association of Individual Investors
625 North Michigan Avenue
Chicago, IL 60611

Includes low-load funds that have a load or fee of 2 percent or less. Provides name of portfolio manager, total return figures, and level of risk involved.

The Handbook for No-Load Fund Investors ($49)
by Sheldon Jacobs
The No-Load Fund Investor, Inc.
Box 318
Irvington, NY 10533

The "bible" of the industry, this annual guide provides advice on selecting the right fund, when to sell, how to switch funds, etc. The *Handbook* with a monthly newsletter that keeps fund investors up-to-date is $139.

So, even if you go the route of a mutual fund, you're still not entirely free of decision making. Now you must, of course, decide which fund you want—there are over 2,000 to choose from! You can narrow your choice, however, by following these steps.

Step 1

Clarify Your Goals. Do you want a fund for income or for growth? Do you want a fund that consists primarily of stocks, bonds, or some of each? Do you want a high-risk speculative fund or a more conservative one? Each fund has different investment objectives, so it is important that you understand these differences before making your selection. The fund's objectives are noted at the beginning of the prospectus, which is the official description of the fund required by the Securities and Exchange Commission. For example, a prospectus might read: "Our primary objective is safety of principal and long-term growth through the purchase of high-quality stocks in growth areas of the economy."

(To order a fund's prospectus simply call the fund's 800 number.)

MUTUAL FUND LOADS

Some mutual funds have no fees, some have low loads (fees), and others outrageously high fees. Here are the key terms you need to know before investing in any mutual fund:

- Front-end load. A sales commission charged when you purchase shares in a fund. These sales fees may be as high as 8.5 percent but most are 4 to 5 percent. The load compensates brokers or salespeople who sell the funds. So if you put $1,000 in a fund with a 5 percent load, only $950 goes to work for you in the fund; the rest goes to a broker or salesperson.

- Back-end load. A fee imposed when you sell shares. A typical back-end load fund charges 6 percent if you redeem shares the first year, 5 percent the second, and so on until the charge disappears completely. If you're forced to sell your shares before the load disappears, it can be an expensive experience.

- Redemption fee. Not to be confused with a back-end load, this fee is charged by some fund companies to discourage frequent trading. The fee is typically charged only to those who sell within a year of investing in the fund and the money is returned to the fund.

- 12b-1 fee. Named after the section of law that authorized it, this fee forces shareholders to pay some of the fund's sales and advertising expenses. It can be as high as 1.25 percent of assets, or $1.25 for every $100 you invest. Even no-load funds can charge 12b-1 fees—up to 0.25 percent per year. Unlike other fund charges, this fee continues every year you own shares of the fund.

- No-load. No sales commission when you purchase shares. Sold directly to the public by the mutual fund company rather than through a sales force of stockbrokers.

➤ Hint: The number of funds charging a front-end load has declined recently and at the same time 12b-1 fees have become far more common. By reducing or cutting out front-end loads, the fund seems to be more like a no-load and easier to sell to the public. Now you know better.

Step 2

Study the Types of Funds. Funds fall into several broad categories. Because of the boom in mutual funds over the past few years, you can select today from a broad range. There are funds that emphasize growth, others that focus on income. Some have tax-free holdings, others aim at capital appreciation or have speculative holdings. In selecting a fund, be realistic about how much time you can afford to spend watching it go up and down. The more speculative its portfolio, the more you need to keep your eye on it in order to know when to get out when its value starts to fall. (See Chapter 5, pages 29–30 for information about funds that invest in derivatives.)

Among some of the basic types of funds are:

- **Growth Funds.** These seek long-term capital appreciation by buying stocks in companies that will grow faster than the rate of inflation. Dividend payments are usually low. Within this category there are the following:

  1) **Aggressive or speculative funds.** These also seek maximum profit, but at a fast rate, which is often achieved by taking greater risks, by selling short, or even by borrowing money for additional leverage. These are also known as maximum capital gains funds.
  2) **Industry funds.** These specialize in one type of stock, such as energy or health care stocks; also called sector funds
  3) **Income Funds.** These invest primarily in corporate bonds and are not concerned with growth. Some invest in high-dividend stocks. For more on bond income funds, see pages 79 and 81–82.
  4) **Balanced Funds.** These maintain portfolios that combine common and preferred stocks and bonds. Their aim is to conserve the investor's principal, to pay current income, and to have long-term growth. These portfolios often consist of leading companies that pay high dividends.

5) **Growth and Income Funds.** Invest in common stock of companies that have had increasing share value and a solid record of paying dividends.
6) **Municipal Bond Funds.** These are designed for tax-exempt income.
7) **U.S. Government Income Funds.** Invest in a variety of government securities: U.S. Treasury bonds, federally guaranteed mortgage-backed securities, and other government notes.
8) **Money Market Funds.**
9) **Specialized Funds.** We will not discuss these funds, for they tend to be very speculative in nature and are not generally appropriate for the under $5,000 investor. If you are interested in any of them, your broker can help you find the best. They include option funds, hedge funds, global and international funds, venture capital funds, and gold funds.

Step 3

Study Management's Performance Record. Rating services provide the performance records of mutual funds over various time periods. These results appear in several financial publications including *Barron's*, *Money*, *Your Money*, and *Kiplinger's Personal Finance Magazine*. Then, read in detail about specific funds in *Morningstar Mutual Funds*, which covers 1,200 mutual funds, although not money market funds, and rates them on the basis of total return, volatility, and performance. It also gives information on each fund's manager. Updated every two weeks. Contact: Morningstar, 225 West Wacker Drive, Chicago, IL 60606; $395/year; 3 month trial: $55. (These and other publications are available at your library or broker's office.)

➤**Hint:** Take advantage of funds' 800 numbers. They're not just there to make transferring from one fund to another easy. Many mutual funds train service reps to answer prospective investor's questions about the fund's portfolio holdings and risk level as well as to provide shareholders with updated information about everything from current share prices to strategies.

Finally, select a fund that is part of a family of funds so you can switch your shares when the market, interest rates, or your goals change.

All in the Family

Even after you have selected a fund, you may be nervous about how it will react to sudden changes in the economy, interest rates, or the market. One way to resolve this dilemma is to keep your money in a family of funds that offers more than one type of fund under the same corporate roof—for example, T. Rowe Price, Fidelity, Vanguard. You should look for a fund family that has a bond fund, a stock fund, and a money market fund so that you can switch your money from one fund to another as the economic climate changes. Pick a fund in which switching is free of charge or offered at a very nominal amount. The prospectus will tell you if you are limited to a certain number of switches per year. Make certain, too, that you can do your switching over the telephone.

How do you know when to switch? It requires time and study, but in general:

- When interest rates fall, keep your money in a mutual fund that has a stock portfolio.
- When interest rates rise, switch to a money market fund or Treasury fund.
- When you see the price of the equities held in your fund going down, switch to a money market fund; park your money here until you have a sense of where the economy is headed.

➤ **Hint:** No one fund should be regarded as economically viable for all times. The market is cyclical, constantly changing, so never make an investment and think that's it. You must continually monitor all investments, including mutual funds.

For help in switching among a family of funds, you may want to examine one of the newsletters that advises readers on how and when to move among the various mutual funds. Ask for a sample copy before taking on a full subscription.

Telephone Switch Newsletter
($137/year; monthly)
2100 Main Street
Huntington Beach, CA 92647
800-950-8765

Mutual Fund Investing
($100/year; monthly)
7811 Montrose Road
Potomac, MD 20854
800-722-9000

The No-Load Fund Investor
($139 includes *Handbook*)
P.O. Box 318
Irvington, NY 10533
800-252-2042

Buying from the Bank

You can purchase mutual funds in over 1800 banks nation-wide. It certainly seems an easy and convenient way to take advantage of one-stop shopping. But there are a few things the investor should know.

Currently, 115 of the funds being sold are proprietary. That is, they are owned and operated by the bank, and experts believe that many of these funds are not expertly managed.

More alarming, when investors purchase a bank mutual fund, many of them assume that it, like their money market deposit account or CD, is FDIC insured. Just because you buy a mutual fund from an FDIC-insured bank doesn't mean the funds they sell are similarly insured. They're not. Although some banks offer a

GROWTH MUTUAL FUNDS

The largest category of equity funds, these tend to outperform most other types of stock funds over the long term. They are best for investors willing to assume a moderate degree of risk and who can hold their shares at least two years, preferably longer.

- Columbia Growth 800-547-1707
- Franklin Growth 800-342-5236
- Guardian Park Avenue 800-221-3253
- Lindner Fund 314-727-5305
- Sogen International 800-334-2143

SIX LOW-RISK FUNDS FOR INCOME

- Benham Adjustable Rate Government Securities Fund 800-472-3389
  Yield will rise when interest rates rise
- Lindner Dividend Fund 314-727-5305
  Utility stocks, corporate bonds, and government debt
- Neuberger & Berman Maturity Bond Fund 800-877-9700
  Short maturities keep shares from fluctuating and income high
- Stratton Monthly Dividend 800-634-5726
  Contains stocks, convertibles; impressive returns
- Strong Short-Term Bond 800-368-1030
  Substantial yields with low risk
- Vanguard Intermediate Term U.S. Treasury Portfolio 800-662-7447
  High quality holdings

variety of funds, some proprietary and some not, the salesperson may receive a larger commission if they sell the bank's proprietary fund to you. And this fund may not necessarily be the one that best suits your investment needs.

Some of the bank proprietary mutual funds have done very well. Others, including some run by major banks, have not. Don't assume that because you're bank is offering a fund or because the bank is nationally recognized that you don't have to do your homework. You still must study the fund's track record, look into its portfolio, and feel assured that it's being expertly managed in a way that fits your needs. When you're purchasing a mutual fund, the convenience of one-stop shopping is not a sufficient reason to invest in a bank-offered mutual fund.

Stock Mutual Funds

Buying shares in an equity fund is often a good alternative to trying to pick from among the thousands of publicly traded individual stocks. For the small investor, the new investor, and the very busy investor, mutual funds offer diversity, professional management, liquidity, relatively low cost, and income and/or price appreciation. Some funds have no minimum investment amount; for others it is as low as $500 and as high as $25,000.

You should have at least $2,000 before you participate in a fund for stocks, however, because in this type of investment there is a greater degree of risk than in money market mutual funds, CDs, and other vehicles we have already described. After all, the stock market, and your fund, could go down, not up, in price. That is the risk you take when purchasing a stock fund.

FUNDS THAT HAVE NOT LOST MONEY

Of the approximately 1,200 stock funds, these have posted earnings gains every year since 1978.

- Phoenix Growth 800-243-4361
- Merrill Lynch Capital A Growth & Income 800-637-3863
- Investment Co. of America Growth & Income 800-421-9900
- John Hancock Sovereign Growth & Income 800-225-5291
- CGM Mutual Balanced 800-345-4048

TOP PERFORMING MUTUAL FUND WINNERS

Stock Funds:

- Aggressive growth: MIM Stock Appreciation 800-233-1240
  No load; $100 minimum initial investment
- Growth & income: Monetta 800-666-3882
  No load; $250 minimum initial investment
- Long-term growth: Berger One Hundred 800-333-1001
  No load; $250 minimum initial investment

Bond Funds:

- High-yield corporate: Kemper Investment Portfolio Diversified Income 800-621-1048
  No sales fee; 4% declining redemption fee; $1,000 minimum
- Top grade tax-exempt: Alliance Municipal Income National 800-221-5672
  4.25% sales fee; $500 minimum
- High-yield tax-exempt: MetLife State Street Tax Exempt 800-882-0052
  4.5% sales fee; $500 minimum
- Government securities: MetLife State Street Gov't Securities 800-882-0052
  4.5% sales fee; $500 minimum

Ginnie Mae Funds

These funds aim for high income and minimum risk and more often than not succeed. Ginnie Maes, short for Government National Mortgage Association (GNMA), are actually pools of mortgages backed by the Federal Housing Administration (FHA) or the Veterans Administration (VA). They are the only securities—except for those issued by the U.S. Treasury—whose principal and interest are backed by the "full faith and credit of the U.S. government."

STOP *Caution:* The guarantee by the government protects you from only one thing: default by homeowners. In other words, it guarantees that interest and principal will be paid—but it guarantees neither the value of fund shares nor the interest rate. Your shares will indeed fluctuate in price, for like bond funds, when interest rates rise the value of Ginnie Mae mutual funds falls, and vice versa. (That's why you should buy Ginnie Mae mutual funds only if you can hold your shares long term, thus smoothing out the fluctuations in interest rates.)

→**Hint:** You can buy a Ginnie Mae certificate for $25,000 through a broker and avoid the problem of fluctuating mutual fund share prices.

A Ginnie Mae begins when a home buyer receives, from a lending institution, a mortgage insured by the FHA or VA. The lender then combines this mortgage with many others into a pool worth at least $1 million. This certificate—a mortgage-backed security—is then sold to a broker, who in turn sells pieces of it, known as certificates, to individual investors and mutual funds. The minimum amount is $25,000. As the homeowners make monthly payments on their loans, owners of certificates receive a share of the principal and interest payments on a monthly basis. Although these are suitable for investors seeking a steady stream of income, *they have one problem:* When interest rates fall, homeowners rush to pay off their mortgages ahead of schedule and refinance at lower rates. When that happens, investors who own certificates receive their principal and interest payments sooner than planned. They then face the problem of reinvesting this money at the then prevailing rates, which of course are lower than when they purchased their certificates.

A Ginnie Mae fund operates quite differently from the certificates. You purchase shares of the fund. The fund manager buys and sells Ginnie Mae certificates in much the same way a bond fund trades bonds. Therefore, *your yield is not fixed* in a fund. It will rise and fall in relation to interest rates. Your fund's success also depends on the ability of the manager to buy and sell certificates at the best time.

STOP *Caution:* Some funds allow a percentage of their portfolio to be invested in slightly riskier real-estate-backed securities such as Freddie Macs, Fannie Maes, or nonguaranteed mortgages in order to keep their yields high. Others remain cautious and invest only in Ginnie Mae certificates and Treasury bonds. A fund's prospectus will spell out these details for you.

Before selecting a fund, read the prospectus to learn what's in the fund's portfolio, if it has check-writing privileges, if it charges for dividend reinvestment, and what its sales fees and other charges are, if any.

GINNIE MAES

For Whom

- Investors who want a high yield

Where to Purchase

- Directly from fund or through stockbrokers

Fee

- Load funds charge a sales fee that ranges from 3 percent to 8.5 percent
- No-load funds do not charge a sales fee, but there may be other hidden costs

Safety

- Relatively high, especially if held long-term

Minimum

- $1,000 for funds, $25,000 for certificates

Advantages

- Yields tend to be slightly higher than U.S. Treasury issues
- Provide income on monthly basis
- Can reinvest income in additional fund shares

Disadvantages

- Fund yields are not guaranteed and could fall
- Some funds are allowed to sell options against their portfolios to keep the yields high; this adds to the risk level
- Price of a fund's shares can drop

14

Socially Conscious Mutual Funds

Is it possible to be a successful investor and socially responsible at the same time? Yes. A growing number of "socially conscious" mutual funds allow investors to reconcile their desire for profits with concern about environmental, political, and social issues. Unlike most mutual funds, which base their portfolios primarily on financial considerations, these funds apply other criteria, called social screens, as well.

Although each fund's screen differs, most refuse weapons manufacturers and utilities that rely on nuclear power. Some screen out the so-called sin stocks: tobacco, liquor, and gambling. Most reject companies that are heavy polluters, and others screen out those that use animals for testing or that lack a strong policy of hiring and promoting women and minorities.

➤**Hint:** Because there is no universal standard for screening portfolios, you must check with individual funds regarding their positions on issues and their specific holdings.

Here are some picks in various categories:

Growth Funds

These invest in stocks expected to provide long-term capital appreciation for shareholders; they have more volatile price swings than the more conservative income or balanced funds described below.

- Dreyfus Third Century 800-645-6561
- New Alternatives 516-466-0808
- Pioneer Capital Growth 800-225-6292
- Parnassus Fund 800-999-3505

Income Funds

- Calvert Social Investment Bond Fund 800-368-2748
- Pioneer Bond Fund 800-225-6292

Balanced Funds

These funds seek the highest possible return consistent with a low-risk strategy. Their portfolios contain both stocks and bonds. They typically have higher dividend yields than growth funds and perform better when stocks are falling in price. In a rising market, however, they usually do not keep pace with growth funds.

- Pax World 800-767-1729
- Calvert Social Investment Managed Growth 800-368-2748

Money Market Funds

These funds do not invest in U.S. Treasury issues because, they maintain, those issues are used primarily to finance a federal deficit largely caused by heavy defense spending. Instead, these funds buy issues of the Federal Farm Credit System and other government agencies.

- Working Assets 800-533-3863
- Calvert Money Fund 800-368-2748

If you're serious about doing well by doing good and investing in funds that satisfy your financial goals and social concerns, get a copy of "Social Investment Forum Guide," which lists stockbrokers and financial planners who screen recommended investments for their social consciousness; cost $45 from: Social Investment Forum, Box 57216, Washington, D.C. 20012, 202-833-5522.

15

Treasuries for Safe Income

When you have accumulated an extra $1,000 or more, it's time to consider one of the safest of all investment vehicles—**Treasuries,** which is Wall Street-ese for securities issued by the U.S. Government. Long regarded as an ideal place for a portion of anyone's savings, these investments have three things in their favor:

- They are the safest form of investment because the U.S. Government guarantees to pay you back.
- They are extremely liquid and can be sold at any time.
- Interest earned is exempt from state and local taxes.

Where do Treasuries come from? Uncle Sam constantly borrows money, not only to finance building battleships but also to cover the high federal deficit, by issuing or selling short-term Treasury bills and longer-term notes and bonds to investors. (The difference among all three—bills, notes, and bonds—is the time limit or maturity. They run from a minimum of thirteen weeks to a maximum of thirty years.)

- **Treasury bills** mature in a year or less. They come in 13-, 26-, and 52-week maturities and require a minimum investment of $10,000. Instead of paying interest, they are sold below face value—that is, at a discount.
- **Hint:** If you don't have $10,000 to put directly in T-bills, consider a Treasury-only money market fund, such as Benham's Capital Preservation which has a minimum investment of $1,000. Call 800-472-3389 for a prospectus.
- **Treasury notes** mature in two to ten years and require a minimum investment of $5,000 for those maturing in less than four years, and $1,000 for those maturing in more than four years.

- **Treasury bonds** mature in ten years or more; the minimum investment is $1,000.

New issues of Treasuries are sold by the government at periodic auctions. Older issues are sold through stockbrokers in what is called the "secondary market."

Bond Basics

Before we go any further, let's find out how bonds actually work. This information applies to bonds issued by the U.S. Treasury, by corporations, and by municipalities.

Simply stated, a bond (unlike a stock) is an IOU. When you purchase a bond you are, in effect, lending your money to the issuing company or government agency. Bonds come in three types:

1) Those issued by the U.S. Government and its agencies
2) Those issued by corporations
3) Those issued by states and municipalities, known as tax-exempt or "munis"

The issuers of the bond are obligated to pay back the full purchase price at a particular time and not before. This is called the **maturity date**.

In general, bonds fall into two time-related categories: *intermediate notes*, which mature in two to ten years; and *long-term bonds*, which mature or come due in ten years or longer.

Until your bond matures, you will receive a fixed rate of interest on your money. This is called the **coupon rate** and is usually paid out twice a year. For example, on a $1,000 bond that pays 8 percent, you receive a $40 check every six months until maturity.

You may be interested to know that the term *coupon* dates from the time when all bonds actually came with a page of attached coupons. On each specified date, the owner of the bond clipped off the coupon, took it to the bank and exchanged it for cash.

The **face value** or denomination of a bond is also known as *par* *value* and is usually $1,000. That means bonds are sold at $1,000 when first issued. After that their price will vary, moving up and down just as stocks do (see below). Depending upon the prevailing market conditions, bonds sell at either *above par* (that is, above $1,000), which is also called *at premium*; or *below par* (that is, less than $1,000) and also called *at a discount.*

And, just to make it a bit more confusing, although bonds are issued and sold in $1,000 units, their prices in the newspaper are quoted on the basis of $100, not $1,000. So you must always add a zero to the published price. For example, a bond quoted at $105 is really selling for $1,050.

The Secondary Market

After bonds have been issued they rise and fall in price depending upon supply and demand and upon the availability of new bonds that give buyers a higher rate or a lower rate. If new bonds pay more interest, then older bonds drop in price. If new bonds pay less interest, then older bonds rise in price because they are more desirable.

You can sell your bond before maturity in the secondary market through a stockbroker—but it is possible you will not receive what you paid for it, the price being more or less dependent upon the market as explained next.

Buying Treasuries

Treasuries are sold through auctions held periodically by the U.S. Treasury for major banks and government bond dealers. The public may also participate (we will tell you how in a bit). These large buyers determine the final interest rate; in other words, no one knows what rate a Treasury issue will pay until the end of the auction.

How You Can Become Part of the Auction

Many people find it simplest to buy Treasuries through a broker and pay the $25 to $35 per bond fee. Yet there's no need to pay this fee because you can also buy Treasuries at the government auctions either through the mail or in person from the Federal Reserve Bank in your area, or the Bureau of Public Debt. When you do, there is absolutely no fee involved. There are twelve Federal Reserve districts, each with a main bank and thirty-six additional branches (see list on pages 92–93).

Dates for Treasury auctions are always announced in advance. The *Wall Street Journal* and other newspapers provide this information or you can call your district Federal Reserve office and get a copy of their newsletter, *Highlights of Treasury Offerings*, which contains a list of auction dates.

The auctions have a regular schedule for the most part. In general:

- 13- and 26-week bills are auctioned every Monday.
- 52-week bills are auctioned once a month.
- 2-year notes are auctioned once a month.
- 3-year and longer notes are auctioned every three months.
- Bonds are auctioned every three months.

Bidding

At the auctions, the Treasury sells its securities on both a competitive and a noncompetitive basis. Competitive sales are made almost entirely to professional traders and institutions. These "big guns," such as banks and bond brokers, put in their bids, stating the yields at which they are willing to buy the Treasury's specific issue. The average individual, however, should enter a noncompetitive bid. In this type of bid, you simply order securities without stating a yield. Your request is then filled at the average of all the accepted competitive bids. (*Note:* Bids are in yields, not price.)

A noncompetitive bid must be postmarked no later than the

day before the auction and received on or before the auction date.

You can also go in person to the nearest Federal Reserve office with your bid by 1 P.M. Eastern time on the day of the auction and make your purchase there. Arrive early, however, as lines can be long, especially when interest rates are high.

Regardless of whether you buy in person or through the mail, you must fill out an order form, known as a tender. This one-page form is available from all Federal Reserve Banks and their branches. On the form there's a place to check the type of bid you wish to make: competitive or noncompetitive. You'll also need to fill in your name, address, and Social Security number, as well as a telephone number where you can be reached during the day.

You can pay with cash, a cashier's check, or a certified personal check. Make certain the check is payable to the specific Federal Reserve Bank from which you are purchasing your Treasury security.

Finally, you must fill in information that enables the interest and principal payments from the Treasuries you are buying to be deposited directly into your bank or financial institution. You will see a line for "routing number." This is simply the nine-digit number that appears on the lower left of your personal check. Next comes the name of the financial institution to which payments will be made, your account number at that institution, the type of account (savings, checking, etc.), and the name of the account holder.

Sign the form, date it, and submit it to the Federal Reserve Bank or branch in your area, or, if you live in the Washington, DC area, to the Bureau of Public Debt, Securities Transaction Branch, Washington, DC 20239.

Treasury Direct System

All sales of Treasuries are recorded on a book-entry basis electronically through what is called the Treasury Direct System. You do not receive a certificate showing ownership of your Treasury as was the case before the age of the computer. The Treasury Direct

System is designed for investors who plan to hold their securities until maturity.

⟶**Hint:** If you need to sell before maturity, you must transfer your Treasuries out of the Treasury Direct System into the commercial book-entry system. To do this, set up an account with a stockbroker or a bank that will sell them for you, for a fee. To transfer your notes or bonds, fill out Form PD5179, "Security Transfer Request," available from any Federal Reserve Bank or branch. In other words to sell Treasuries, you must use a broker or a bank that offers this service.

⟶**Hint:** If you know you will not be holding your Treasuries until they mature, buy them from a broker or bank. This automatically puts you in the commercial book-entry system from the beginning.

The Secondary Market

Treasuries can also be purchased in the secondary market. These issues result from the fact that an investor who purchased a Treasury now wants to sell it. To buy in the secondary market you must use a broker. The commission varies and depends somewhat on how many Treasuries you are trading. Some charge $25 to $35 or more for orders of any size. Others charge a flat fee—maybe $50, $75, or $100, regardless of the size of the order. Most brokers buy Treasuries primarily as a service to their clients, because they do not make much on the transaction.

Many discount brokers will also buy Treasuries. It's worth calling several discount brokers in your area because the cost to you will be much lower than with a full-service broker.

THE TWELVE FEDERAL RESERVE BANKS

Boston	**New York**
600 Atlantic Avenue	33 Liberty Street
Boston, MA 02106	New York, NY 10045
617-973-3810	212-720-6619

Richmond
701 East Byrd Street
Richmond, VA 23219
804-697-8000
Philadelphia
100 North Sixth Street
Philadelphia, PA 19106
215-574-6675
Dallas
2200 North Pearl Street
Dallas, TX 75201
214-922-6100
St. Louis
411 Locust Street
St. Louis, MO 63101
314-444-8703
Cleveland
1455 East Sixth Street
Cleveland, OH 44101
216-579-2490

Atlanta
104 Marietta Street NW
Atlanta, GA 30303
404-521-8653
Chicago
230 South La Salle Street
Chicago, IL 60690
312-322-5369
Minneapolis
250 Marquette Avenue
Minneapolis, MN 55480
612-340-2075
Kansas
925 Grand Blvd.
Kansas City, MO 64198
816-881-2409
San Francisco
101 Market Street
San Francisco, CA 94105
415-974-2330

U.S. TREASURIES

For Whom

- Investors seeking absolute safety
- Those with a minimum of $1,000
- Those who enjoy helping Uncle Sam

Fee

- There is no fee if purchased directly from the Federal Reserve.
- Banks and brokers charge fees ranging from $25 to as high as $50 or $75.

Safety Factor

- The highest possible
- Backed by the U.S. Government

Advantages

- Principal and interest are guaranteed against default.
- Maximum liquidity
- The state and local tax exemption on interest earned makes Treasuries especially attractive for those who live in a state with high taxes.

Disadvantages

- Troublesome to purchase unless you pay the fee and use a broker.
- Competitive bidding on Treasuries is a skilled art and should not be attempted by the average investor.
- Since you have to pay the Treasury in advance of the auction, you will lose some interest if your money was in an interest-bearing account.
- Buying a bank CD is easier, generally pays about the same interest or a little less, but interest on a CD is fully taxable.

TREASURY TELEPHONE HELP

Call: 202-874-4000. A recorded message with general information on how to buy Treasuries by mail and a listing of other important data and telephone numbers. At the end of the recorded announcement, an analyst will answer your specific questions.

Most of the Federal Reserve Banks listed in this chapter have recorded announcements with similar details. Pamphlets and other material on Treasuries are available from: Bureau of the Public Debt, 200 Third Street, Parkersburg, VA 26106.

You may also be interested in the following publications:

Basic Information on Treasury Bills (free)
Federal Reserve Bank of New York
Issues Division
33 Liberty Street

New York, NY 10045
212-720-6619

Buying Treasury Securities at Federal Reserve Banks ($4.50)
Federal Reserve Bank of Richmond
Public Services Department
P.O. Box 27622
Richmond, VA 23262
804-697-8000

U.S. Financial Data ($21/year; weekly newsletter)
Federal Reserve Bank of St. Louis
P.O. Box 66953
St. Louis, MO 63166
314-444-8808

Grant's Interest Rate Observer ($495/year; semimonthly)
30 Wall Street
New York, NY 10005
212-809-7994

PART FIVE

When You Have $5,000

16

Bonds: Corporates, Munis, & Zeros

In Chapter 15 we discussed bonds issued by the U.S. Treasury as the ultimate, safe choice for steady income. There are two other categories of bonds that also offer income: **corporate bonds** and **municipal bonds**. Corporates pay slightly higher rates than Treasuries and they're slightly higher in risk. On the other hand, municipal bonds, whose yields are lower, have the great advantage of paying tax-exempt income at the federal level and in many cases, at the state and local levels as well.

Both corporate and municipal bonds pay a set rate of interest twice a year for the life of the bond and, if you hold the bonds until maturity you'll get back the face value—$1,000 per bond.

Most brokerage firms have a minimum bond investment of at least $5,000 or $10,000. Yet it is possible to buy a single $1,000 bond through a stockbroker—but the commission is likely to eat into any potential profit. Many experts argue that a bond portfolio with less than $100,000 is not sufficiently diversified to protect against defaults and calls. For all these reasons, if you have a small amount to invest, you're far better off buying shares in a bond mutual fund or a unit investment trust. These two vehicles are explained on pages 103–109.

How to Select Bonds

Credit Risk

Before purchasing a corporate or a municipal bond, take time to determine the issuer's credit-worthiness as given by either Standard & Poor's or Moody's—the two independent rating services. Both publications, periodically updated, are available at most public libraries and brokers' offices. The highest rating a bond can receive is triple A. Medium-grade bonds fall into the triple B category, while those that are C or lower are speculative. In general, inexperienced and conservative investors should stick with bonds rated A or better.

A bond's yield also reflects the issuer's credit quality. Lower quality bonds, also known as non-investment grade—those rated BB or below, generally have higher yields than better quality issues. The higher yield compensates the investor for lending money to a company that is considered somewhat likely to default on its interest or principal payments.

In addition to the credit risk or financial shape of the corporation or municipality, there are two additional risk factors to bear in mind when investing in bonds: interest rate risk and the call factor.

- **Interest rate risk** is a problem for those who sell bonds prior to maturity. If you sell and interest rates have climbed since your purchase, your bond may very well be worth less than when you bought it. That's because newly issued bonds, paying the new, higher rates, are more prized.

Moody's		S&P
Aaa	Top quality	AAA
Aa	Excellent	AA
A	Very high	A
Baa	Medium	BBB
Ba	Speculative	BB
B	Lower speculative	B
Caa	Poor & risky	CCC
Ca	Near default	CC
C	In default	C

Of course, the opposite is also true: if rates fall your bond will be worth more because it is still paying the old, higher rate.

- Your bonds may be "called in—" taken away from you. Most bonds have **call features**, which give the issuer the right to redeem the bond before maturity. You receive the full face value of the bond, but of course you then face the problem of investing that money at the prevailing rate, which is usually lower than the one you were receiving. The conditions for calling in a bond are provided in the statement filed with the SEC when the bonds are first issued to the public. Call features are also listed in the bond guides.

The call feature is usually not exercised if the current interest rate is the same as or higher than the bond coupon rate. But if interest rates fall below the bond coupon rate, the bond may be called because the issuer can now borrow money at a lower rate. The issuer, in fact, may issue new bonds at this lower rate. (Remember, a bond is just a loan you make to the issuer, who would naturally prefer to pay the lowest interest rate possible.)

Call Protection

If a bond is called in, you then lose that steady stream of income you thought you had locked in for a given number of years. But there is a way to protect yourself from calls, and it is especially essential when investing long term. You can buy a bond with "call protection," which guarantees that it will not be called for a specific number of years. Corporate bonds are likely to offer ten-year call protection. Most government bonds are not callable at all, but check carefully; some, contrary to popular thinking, are.

Corporate Bonds

Thousands of U.S. corporations raise money by selling bonds to the public. Some of these companies are small and obscure; others are well known. In general, it is best to stick to the bonds of leading companies and those that are traded on the New York Stock Exchange. Then, if you need to sell them to raise cash, you can do so more easily than if you own obscure issues.

Bond prices are listed in the financial pages of the newspaper. They are quoted with fractions listed in eighths. For example, a bond listed at $98-1/4 is really selling for $982.50. Here's what a typical listing looks like:

Bond	Current Yield	Sales in $1,000	High	Low	Last	Net Change
duPont 6-$^1/_2$ 06	6.97	39	93-$^3/_8$	92-$^3/_4$	93-$^1/_4$	+$^1/_8$

The first column indicates that this E.I. duPont Corporation bond has a coupon rate of 6.5 percent and a maturity date of 2006. In other words, it pays $65 per year for every $1,000 bond. If you divide the coupon rate (6.5 percent) by the current market price (which is listed under "Last" and is $93-1/4), you will get the current yield (which is 6.97 percent). The volume of bonds traded was 39 bonds. The high was $93.375 and the low $92.75. The closing price was $93.25, up $12.50 per bond.

You may wonder why the yield for this bond rose from 6.5 percent to 6.97 percent. The answer is that the price of the bond has gone down from $1,000, which it was on the first day it was issued, to $932.50.

Are Corporate Bonds Right for You?

Yes, if you stay with top rated, financially solid corporations, such as Xerox, IBM, duPont, Eastman Kodak, Bristol-Myers Squibb and many public utility companies. But remember, unlike Treasury bills, notes, and bonds, corporate bonds are not guaranteed or backed by the government. Corporate bond issuers can and have defaulted. Your protection is the financial strength of the corporation. And, *the greater the financial strength of the issuer, the lower the coupon or interest rate, because safety is traded off for lower yields.*

➤**Hint:** If you live in a high tax state, factor in the tax advantage of Treasury issues when considering corporate bonds. Income earned on Treasuries is subject to federal income tax but not state and local taxes. And remember that corporates can be used to fund self-directed IRAs, SEPs, and Keoghs—plans that defer taxes on their earnings.

A Corporate Bond Portfolio

- General Electric 7.17% coupon, due 1997
- Exxon 6-1/2% coupon, due 1998
- Commonwealth Edison 8-3/4% coupon, due 2005
- Dow Chemical 8-1/2% coupon, due 2005
- Bell Tel of PA 8-1/4% coupon, due 2017

(*Note:* The owner of these bonds will receive his return of principal staggered over four different years, starting in 1997 and ending in 2017. This technique, called laddering, can also be done with CDs. It is particularly effective for meeting college tuition bills, retirement needs, or other specific financial goals.)

CORPORATE BONDS

For Whom

- Anyone seeking high fixed income who also accepts the risk of changing interest-rates
- Best for those who can hold their bonds until maturity in order to get back the bonds' full face value

Safety Factor

- Can be determined by bond ratings, with AAA and AA being the highest ratings
- Varies depending upon the corporation
- Are not insured or guaranteed

Minimum Investment

- $1,000 (Many brokers have a $5,000 minimum)

Advantages

- Corporate bonds almost always pay higher interest rates than government bonds or those issued by municipalities
- You can select bonds to come due when you need an influx of money
- A sound way to get a steady stream of income

Disadvantages

- Many bonds have call provisions
- If you sell before maturity you may get back less than you paid
- Interest income is subject to federal, state, and local taxes
- There is generally minimal appreciation of your principal, whereas with many stocks, investors benefit from significant increases in the price of their shares

Corporate Bond Mutual Funds

Small investors and those who lack experience in selecting individual bonds are often better off investing through a corporate bond mutual fund. Here the bonds are professionally selected and managed.

Fund	Minimum Investment	Telephone
Laurel Managed Income	$1,000	800-225-5267
Dean Witter		
Intermediate Income	1,000	800-869-3863
T. Row Price Short		
Term Bond	2,500	800-638-5660
Vanguard Bond Market	3,000	800-662-7447

Municipal Bonds

Municipal bonds, also known as tax-exempts, are a good choice for investors in the 28 percent tax bracket seeking tax-free income. "Munis" as they are called on Wall Street, are issued by cities, counties, states, and special agencies to finance various projects. Their biggest plus: Interest paid is exempt from federal income tax and state and local taxes to residents of the area where issued.

🛑 *Caution*: If you buy municipals outside the state where you are a resident, their interest income will be subject to taxes in your state. And, any capital gains made in selling municipals is subject to all federal and most state tax laws.

Because of their tax advantage, municipal bonds pay lower interest rates than comparable corporate bonds or government securities. In other words, yields on corporates and Treasuries represent the return before taxes are paid on the income generated. The interest and principal are repaid to you from the taxes and revenues collected by the municipality issuing the bonds.

Municipal bond dealers and the major retail brokers such as Merrill Lynch, Paine Webber, and others are primarily interested in working with customers who have a minimum of $15,000 to $25,000 to invest in these bonds. Although you may indeed find brokers who will take smaller orders, the commission will be hefty vis-à-vis your dollar investment. (And mark ups on munis sold through brokers range from 1 to 4%.) Investors with several thousand dollars can still invest by purchasing unit investment trusts or municipal bond funds, explained below.

How to Select Tax-Exempt Bonds

There are three factors to check when considering tax-exempt bonds: *safety*, *yield*, and *liquidity*. You can check the safety of any bond, tax-exempt or not, through Moody's or Standard & Poor's rating services.

In addition to sticking to A-rated bonds, you can increase your safety factor by purchasing bonds that are insured even though their yields are slightly lower than uninsured munis.

Because municipal bonds issuers have occasionally defaulted (the best-known example being the Washington Public Power System), **insured bonds** are a sound idea in today's economic climate.

In order to insure a bond, the issuer pays an insurance company a premium that ranges from 0.1 percent to 2 percent of the bond's total principal and interest. The insurance company then agrees to pay both the principal and the interest to bondholders if the issuer defaults on making these payments. Policies generally last the life of the bond. You will find that insured bonds have slightly lower yields, for obvious reasons. Your broker can tell you which bonds are insured. For additional information on insured municipal bonds, write to:

- Mutual Bond Investors Assurance
  113 King Street
  Armonk, NY 10504
  914-273-4545

- AMBAC Indemnity Corp.
  1 State Street Plaza
  New York, NY 10004
  212-668-0340

The second factor in municipal bond selection is *yield*. Tax-exempts, as we mentioned before, pay lower interest rates than most taxable bonds and therefore are not appropriate for people in low tax brackets or for placement in already tax-deferred retirement accounts, such as an IRA. Yet for investors in high tax brackets, municipal bonds can reap surprisingly good returns. If, for example, you are married, file a joint return, and earn $45,000 annually, you need a yield of 10.76 percent on a taxable investment, such as a corporate bond, to equal a 7.75 percent tax-exempt yield. The table/chart on page 109 shows the relationship between taxed and tax-free income.

You can further boost your return by investing in triple exempt municipals—those in which interest is free from federal, state, and local taxes for residents. Triple-exempts are especially good for people living in states with high income taxes.

The third factor involved in municipal bond selection is *liquidity*; that is, the ability to find someone who wants to buy your bond, should you wish to sell before maturity. It is best to stick with bonds of large, well-known municipalities or state governments. If you want to sell an obligation of the Moorland, Iowa, School District, for example, it may be weeks before you find a dealer willing to buy these obscure bonds.

Note: Municipal bond mutual funds are also very liquid.

Types of Municipal Bonds

- The safest category of munis are called **general obligation bonds**. Sold to help build roads, schools, and government buildings, they are tax-exempt as long as no more than 10 percent of their proceeds goes to a private enterprise. Bonds issued for non-profit organizations are also tax-exempt. GOs have the highest safety ratings because they are backed by the issuer's full taxing and revenue-raising powers.
- **Revenue bonds** depend upon the income earned by a specific project or authority, such as road or bridge tolls, or revenues from a publicly financed hospital.

105

- **Industrial development bonds** are issued to finance facilities that are in turn leased to private corporations. The tax law stipulates that if more than 10 percent of the proceeds raised by their sale is used by private enterprise, the interest a bondholder receives may be subject to a special tax, known as the alternative minimum tax (AMT). The AMT is designed to make sure that Americans with tax-sheltered investments do not escape paying income taxes. ⬣ *Caution:* Before investing in an industrial development bond, check with your accountant to see if you are subject to the AMT; if so, avoid these particular bonds.

➤ **Hint:** Zero coupon municipals are an excellent way to save for a child's education. They are sold at a discount and redeemed in the future at a higher face value. And you never have to pay federal income tax on them. Zeros are explained in full below.

Municipal Bond Mutual Funds & Unit Investment Trusts

If you have only one or two thousand dollars to invest, you are only able to purchase one or two bonds. Putting all your eggs in one basket is not sound planning. As a hedge against the risk of an issuer defaulting, it's wise to hold at least five to ten different bonds and/or buy only insured issues. If you don't have that much money to invest there are two reasonably priced ways to own a diversified muni bond portfolio: mutual funds and unit investment trusts. In both, your risk is spread out through participation in large, diversified portfolios of bonds that are professionally selected.

Municipal Bond Mutual Funds

A municipal bond fund's portfolio is made up of tax-exempt munis—most hold over 100 bonds. The typical minimum investment is $1,000. They operate like any other mutual fund—that is, the portfolio manager buys and sells securities in order to maximize the fund's yield. Unlike a unit investment trust (explained below) where the yield is fixed, a fund's shares fluctuate on a daily basis.

Interest earned is automatically reinvested unless you give directions to the contrary; and an increasing number of bond funds allow you to write checks, usually a minimum of $500, against the value of your shares.

If you ever wish to sell, the fund will buy back your shares at the current market price, which could be more or less than what you originally paid.

MUNICIPAL BOND MUTUAL FUNDS		
	Minimum to Open	
Alliance Municipal Insured National	$250	800-221-5672
Flagship Tax-exempt Limited Term	3,000	800-227-4648
Scudder Medium Term Tax Free	1,000	800-225-2470

Tax-Exempt Unit Investment Trusts

For those who wish to lock in a fixed tax-exempt yield, a **unit investment trust** is ideal. Most require a minimum investment of $1,000 per unit. These prepackaged, diversified portfolios lock in a specific, unchanging yield. Unlike bond mutual funds, they are "unmanaged" and once the bonds for the trust have been selected, no new issues are added. (Issues that turn out to be a problem, however, can be sold in order to minimize losses.) The trust gradually liquidates itself as the bonds mature.

Unit investment trusts are set up by big brokerage houses and bond dealers who buy several million dollars' worth of bonds and then sell them to individual investors in $1,000 pieces. You pay the broker a one-time up-front fee, commonly 4.5 percent. You also pay trustee fees of up to .20 percent a year. A typical unit investment trust holds 20 bonds until maturity unless the bonds are called or defaulted. Most hold bonds maturing in 25 to 30 years, though some are set up to end sooner, and you can buy them with shorter maturities in the secondary market. While you own a trust, you receive tax-free income on a monthly or quarterly basis.

▶**Hint:** Don't be surprised if your checks are not the same every month. As bonds mature or are called, this activity is reflected in your monthly checks.

If you do not wish to hold the trust until maturity, you can sell it in the "secondary market" either to the sponsor or to another broker. What you get back will depend on the market. If interest rates have fallen, you will get more; but if they've gone up, it's possible that you may not even get back your original price.

🛑 *Caution:* Unit investment trusts are not as liquid as mutual funds.

Talk to your broker in order to find out which trusts are available now, and at what price. Be certain to check the rating of the bonds held in the trust. If you're conservative, stick with AAA-rated bonds, or buy an insured trust.

Single-State Investment Trusts & Bond Funds

The best investment for those living in high income tax states is often either a **single-state investment trust** or **mutual fund.** These contain bonds that have a triple tax exemption—that is, they are free from federal, state, and local taxes for residents of that state. Trusts are sold by regional brokers, large brokerage firms, and bond specialists. In addition, two companies sponsor a number of single-state trusts.

Contact them for further information:

- John Nuveen & Company
  333 West Wacker Drive
  Chicago, IL 60606
  312-917-7700

- Van Kampen Merritt
  Mellon Bank Center
  Philadelphia, PA 19103
  800-225-2222

Single state muni mutual bond funds are sold by the mutual fund investment company in the case of no-load funds and by stockbrokers in the case of load funds.

SOME SINGLE STATE MUNI BOND FUNDS

Calif	Scudder Calif Tax Free	800-253-2277
Conn	Fidelity Spartan CT High Yield	800-544-8888
Mass	Putnam MA Tax Exempt Income	800-225-1581
NY	USAA Tax Exempt NY Bond	800-531-8181

STOP *Caution:* These funds lack the diversity of a broadly based national municipal bond fund. If you live in a state with fiscal problems, put no more than half your tax-free portfolio in single state mutual funds or unit investment trusts.

THE TAX-EXEMPT EDGE

Find your tax bracket on the left, then at the top of the table find the tax-exempt yield. Read down to determine the yield you need on a taxable security to equal the yield on a municipal.

Tax-exempt Yield

Tax Bracket	6.5%	7%	7.5%	8%
15%	7.64	8.23	8.82	9.41
28%	9.02	9.72	10.41	11.11
33%	9.70	10.45	11.19	11.94

TAX-EXEMPT UNIT TRUST VS. TAX-EXEMPT BOND MUTUAL FUND

Here are the key differences:

- In a tax-exempt unit trust the portfolio is fixed; no trading activity is conducted after initial bond purchases are made by the trust.
- In a tax-exempt bond fund, investments are continually bought and sold in order to maximize a high tax-exempt income.

- Unit investment trusts are intended to be held to maturity, typically 5 to 30 years.
- Bond mutual funds can be for long- or short-term holding.
- Unit trusts provide regular income checks.
- Bond funds provide income when you sell your shares, although monthly interest income can be sent to you or reinvested.

Zero Coupon Bonds

If you will need money for college tuition, retirement, or to meet some other long-term financial goal, **zero coupon bonds** offer a viable solution, because you make a small investment initially and get a large balloon payment in the future.

A "zero," unlike regular bonds, pays zero interest until maturity. To compensate for this fact, it is sold at a deep discount, well below the $1,000 standard bond price, and it increases in value at a compound rate so that by maturity it is worth much more than when you bought it. Although this type of bond does not pay interest along the way, you will be taxed annually by the IRS as though it did, because the government wants to collect the tax due along the way.

For example, a $1,000 zero that yields 6.2 percent and matures in twenty years sells for only $85.40. In other words, you invest $85.40 at 6.2 percent today; 6.2 percent interest is paid on your investment and the reinvested interest, and after twenty years your $85.40 will equal $1,000. Interest "turns into" principal, and is paid to you in a lump sum upon maturity.

Note: EE Savings Bonds are zeros.

As you can see, with a zero coupon bond you know ahead of time exactly how much money you will have when the bond comes due. Yet because zeros, unlike regular bonds, lock in interest, you get a slightly lower yield, about 1/2 to 1 percentage point below bonds that have a regular coupon.

The most popular types of zeros are:

- **Treasury zeros** are packaged and sold by large brokerage and investment houses. These institutions buy huge lots of long-term U.S. Treasury bonds, clip off (or "strip off") the semiannual interest coupons, then sell these coupons, which come due twice a year during the life of the bond. Each package guarantees that the buyer of these coupons will get $1,000 upon maturity. Principal and interest are guaranteed by the U.S. Government. These "strip bonds," as they are called, are also known by various names: Merrill Lynch sells TIGERs, which stands for Treasury Investment Growth Receipt; Salomon Brothers' CATS are Certificates of Accrual on Treasury Securities and are available through Prudential-Bache; and LIONs, Lehman Investment Opportunity Notes, are sold through Shearson Lehman Hutton.

Recent examples:

1) A six year Treasury zero yielding 6.13 percent sold for $693.20
2) A ten zero yielding 7.17 percent sold for $492.
3) A twenty-two year zero yielding 8.18 percent sold for $173.20
4) **Tax-exempt zeros** are issued by municipalities, states, and other agencies. Just as with other municipal bonds, their interest is exempt from federal income tax and from state and local tax in the issuing community. Like other tax-exempt bonds, they pay a lower rate than non tax-exempts.
5) **Zero coupon CDs** are similar to zero coupon bonds. They are obligations of large banks and, like bank deposits, are insured up to $100,000 by the FDIC.
6) There are a handful of corporate zeros.

How to Build a College Fund with Zeros

A grandmother attending the first birthday celebration of her grand-daughter announced a gift of $10,000 toward the little girl's college education, which would start in 2008. Her cost for this $10,000 was only $1,060, because she had purchased zero coupon bonds from her broker that were due to mature in 2008. You, too, can use zero coupon bonds to prepare for the day when your child or grandchild goes to college.

- Select zeros scheduled to come due at the right time
- Set up a custodial account through your broker or bank. This type of account holds money, stocks, or bonds in a parent's name for the child until he or she is of age. (Unearned income of a child aged 14 or less, regardless of the source, is taxed at the parent's rate when this income exceeds $1,200. But the first $600 is not taxed, and the next $600 is taxed at the child's rate. If the child is over 14, all income is taxed at the child's rate, presumably lower than the parent's.)
- Gifts made by grandparents and relatives other than parents are taxed at the child's (presumably) lower rate, regardless of the child's age.

ZERO COUPON BONDS

For Whom

- Those who know they will need a certain amount of money at a certain time in the future
- Those who can hold bonds until maturity because zero prices fluctuate widely

Minimum

- Typically between $150 and $450, but varies widely

Safety Factor

- Minimal risk

Advantages

- You know precisely how much you must invest now to get a certain amount of money on a certain date in the future
- You do not have to be concerned with the reinvestment of interest payments as is the case with regular bonds

Disadvantages

- When interest rates rise, the value of the zeros you hold falls even more than the value of regular bonds, because, since you have no cash in hand from interest payments, you cannot take a zero's interest and reinvest it at a higher rate elsewhere
- Yields are 1/2 to 1 percentage point below ordinary bonds
- The IRS insists that taxes be paid annually on zero coupon bonds just as if you actually received the interest
- You are paying taxes on theoretical interest even though no cash is received until the date of maturity. The buyer of a regular bond pays taxes, too, but also receives interest payments in the form of cash twice a year

➤**Hint:** If you do not want to get locked into the lower yield of a longer-term zero coupon bond because you fear inflation and the higher interest rates it brings, buy zeros with shorter maturities.

17

A Stock Portfolio for Beginners

Buy stocks that go up, and if they don't, don't buy 'em.
—Will Rogers

Easier said than done. Yet even though stocks go down as well as up, many Americans like owning stocks, owning a piece of American industry. Many actually do more than just think about it—over 20 percent of the U.S. population owns stocks.

According to a recent study done by the Securities Industry Association, individual investors buy and sell an average of 157.6 million shares a day.

There are four compelling reasons why, at the $5,000 level, you too, should consider buying stocks:

- Over the long term, stocks tend to outperform bonds.
- Stocks offer the possibility of price appreciation.
- Stocks offer the possibility of keeping ahead of inflation.
- Stocks, especially those paying high dividends, are also a source of income.

➤**Hint:** If you have never owned a stock, read "What Is a Stock" in Chapter 8.

Are You Ready for the Market?

Prior to selecting stocks for your own portfolio, you must have money set aside for an emergency. At least three months' worth of living expenses should be safely stashed away in a liquid investment, such as a money market mutual fund, a money market deposit account, or a certificate of deposit. Once this has been accomplished and you have accumulated $5,000, you're ready to go. (Although it *is* possible to invest in the market with smaller amounts of money, in order to establish a truly diversified portfolio you need a base of about $5,000.)

First, *determine your investment goals*. Are you seeking a stock that pays a high cash dividend, or would you prefer to buy one that will appreciate substantially in price? Do you want liquidity—that is, the ability to get money back when you want it, or are you content to wait for long-term growth? Your goals make a difference, because no one stock offers high dividends, instant liquidity, spectacular appreciation, plus stability.

The Risk Factor

But, before you invest, keep in mind that while many stocks are profitable investments and return handsome rewards in terms of capital appreciation, they also can decline in price. *There is no guarantee that you will make a profit.* Careful selection is essential.

The ABCs of Stock Selection

When you have accumulated $5,000 *and* established an emergency nest egg, you can prudently consider investing for either growth or income through the purchase of common stocks. A **common stock** is a fractional share of ownership in a corporation. For example, if a corporation has one million outstanding shares and you buy one share, you then own one-millionth of that corporation.

This ownership enables you to participate in the fortunes of the corporation. If the corporation prospers, its earnings (which are expressed as earnings per share) will rise, which in turn tends to make the price of the stock rise. Simply put, the corporation's value has increased. Generally, some part of these earnings is

115

shared with stockholders in the form of a cash dividend that is paid out four times a year.

If you believe that certain corporations or industries will flourish in the coming years, try selecting several common stocks in these areas as an investment for income, growth, or a combination of the two. As a general rule, don't put more than 10 percent of your funds into the stock of any one company and no more than 20 percent in any one industry.

Remember that stocks can also decline in price and you should try to confine your selections primarily to blue chip companies, that is, large, well-financed, and established corporations with secure positions within their industry.

Here are five key standards to use in judging a stock.

1) **Earnings per share should show an upward trend over the previous five years.** If, however, earnings declined for one year out of five, this is acceptable, provided the overall trend continues to rise.

    Earnings per share, simply defined, is the company's net income (after taxes and money for preferred stock dividends) divided by the average number of common stock shares outstanding. You will find it listed in the company's annual report or in professional materials such as *Value Line* or Standard & Poor's *Stock Guide*, available at your library or in any broker's office.

2) **Increasing earnings should be accompanied by similarly increasing dividends.** You should study the cash dividend payments over the previous five-year period. In some cases a corporation will use most of its earnings to invest in future growth, and dividends may be quite modest and rightly so. But even in these cases, some token dividend should be paid annually. Ideally, a company should earn at least $5 for every $4 it pays out.

    In conjunction with the company's dividend, you should note its **yield**, which is the current dividend divided by the price of a share. It is listed in the newspaper along with the dividend and other statistics. The yield should be higher for a stock you purchase for income than for one selected for potential price appreciation (see sample stock listing, later in this chapter).

3) **Standard & Poor's rates each company's financial strength.** For you, the $5,000 investor, the minimum acceptable rating should be A−.

4) **The number of outstanding shares should be at least ten million.** Marketability and liquidity depend upon a large supply of common stock shares. Ten million shares ensures activity by the major institutions, such as mutual funds, pension funds, and insurance companies. Institutional participation helps guarantee an active market in which you and others can readily buy and sell the company's stock.

5) **Study the company's price to earnings ratio (P/E ratio).** This ratio is found by dividing the previous year's earnings per share (or the current year's estimated earnings) into the current price of the stock. The **P/E ratio** is one of the most important analytical tools in the business. It reflects investor opinion about the stock and about the market as a whole. For example, a P/E of 11 means investors are willing to pay 11 times earnings for that stock. A P/E of 11 indicates greater investor interest and confidence than a P/E of 7 or 5, for example.

A P/E ratio under 10 is considered conservative and, depending upon the company, its industry, and your broker's advice, you can feel comfortable with a P/E of 10 or less. As a company's P/E moves above 10, you begin to pay a premium for some aspect of the company's future. For example, a P/E ratio above 10 may very well be justified by outstanding prospects for future growth, by new technological advances, or by worldwide shortages of a product that the company produces.

Basically, the P/E ratio is the measure of the common stock's value to investors. A low P/E of 5 or 6 usually means that the prospects are clouded by uncertainty.

Similarly, a P/E of 14 or 15 indicates a keen appetite on the part of investors to participate in that company's future.

Whatever stock or stocks you decide to buy, you want to get in at the lowest possible P/E—before there is a lot of investor interest and the P/E is bid up. No one can say exactly what ratio you should accept, and it is here that your selection process and your broker's advice become important.

What Stocks Should You Invest In?

- Sound industries that provide basics, such as food or utilities. These tend to hold their own even during recessionary periods.
- Companies that are industry leaders, especially if you are a beginning investor.
- More than one company and more than one industry. If you invest in one company and it turns out to be a mistake, you will have lost everything.
- Stocks listed on the New York or American stock exchanges give you added protection because in order for a stock to be listed the company must file financial statements with the SEC and the stock exchange and meet certain standards. They are also easier to buy and sell.

How to Read a Financial Page

Once you own stocks, you will want to know how they are doing—whether they are going up or down in price. To find out, you can read the market quotations in the daily newspaper.

You will find your stock listed under the name of its exchange—the New York Stock Exchange, American Stock Exchange, Over-the-Counter, and so forth. Here's how it works, using IBM—International Business Machines Corporation—as an example (prices are quoted in fractions of a dollar, so 107-5/8 means $107.675 per share):

52 Week				Yield	P/E	Sales				
High	Low	Stock	Div	%	ratio	100s	High	Low	Last	Chg
123-1/8	93-1/8	IBM	4.84	4.5	15	26586	109	104-5/8	107-5/8	+2-1/4

- The first two columns give the highest and the lowest prices per share for the previous 52 weeks. In the case of IBM, they are 123-1/8 and 93-1/8.
- The next column gives an abbreviated form of the stock's name. Here it is IBM.
- Then comes the annual dividend, if any. For IBM it is $4.84.
- Following the dividend is the stock's yield, which is given as a percentage. To determine the yield, divide the dividend by the closing price: $4.84 divided by $107.675 = 4.5%.
- After the yield comes the P/E ratio or price divided by earnings. You will note that earnings are not listed in the paper. The P/E here is 15.
- The number 26586 in the next column indicates the number of shares traded that particular day. It is listed in hundreds, so 2,658,600 shares of IBM were traded on that day.
- The next two numbers, 109 and 104-5/8 tell how high and how low the stock traded that day. In other words, during the course of the day, some stock traded as high as 109 and some trades were made for as little as 104-5/8 per share. The following column shows the price of the final trade that day, and the final column illustrates the change in the closing price from the prior day. In this case it was 107-5/8, which was 2-1/4 (or $2.25) over the preceding day's closing price. Sometimes there will be a minus sign, indicating it fell in price. If there's no plus or minus sign, then the

closing price was the same as the day before. *Note:* These figures do not include the broker's commission.

Buying Stocks

Once you have decided to become involved with the stock market, the next issue to resolve is whether to use a broker or to select your own stocks. Generally speaking, if you have never owned a stock before, it is probably more prudent to get help from an experienced professional than to go it alone.

Selecting a Broker

Knowing when and how to seek the advice of an expert is a critical part of being a successful investor. If you've never had a broker (or if you've had one you did not like) you can find the right one by doing some investigative work well in advance. Plan on spending three to four weeks to locate the broker who is right for you.

Start by thinking about how you selected your doctor or lawyer. Someone else probably suggested them to you. Getting the recommendations of friends and colleagues whose judgement you respect is one of the best ways to find a good broker. Ask your boss, accountant, banker, uncle, or your pediatrician if they have a broker they like.

After gathering several names, call and make appointments with each one. Tell them the amount of money you have to invest. Not all brokers are interested in small accounts, yet many are. Those who are, realize that a small account obviously has the potential of becoming a larger one over time. A number of the major "full service" houses, such as Merrill Lynch, Paine Webber, and Lehman Bros., are indeed willing to open small accounts. Merrill Lynch has a special program for small investors, described on pages 47–49. You will also find that reliable regional brokers are prepared to handle accounts of all sizes, and they are eager to help local investors. If you feel you don't need investment advice, you can save on commissions by buying through a "discount" broker, such as Charles Schwab, Quick & Reilly, Muriel Siebert, and Olde. In either event, a broker must execute the final buy or sell transaction for you.

Before you interview your broker candidates, prepare a list of questions to ask them. It should include these four items, plus anything else that concerns you:

1) *Do you handle accounts of this size?* You certainly don't want to use a broker who is uninterested in $5,000.
2) *Can you give me one or two references?* Avoid any broker who says no.
3) *How long have you been a broker?* Any broker tends to look great in a good market. You want an experienced person who knows how to handle money in bad times as well as good.
4) *How should I invest my $5,000?* Beware of the broker who advises you to put it all in one stock, or even all in the market. Unless you have specifically said the total amount is to be invested in stocks, the broker should advise you to diversify.

For additional details on how to select a broker you may want to check with your library for a copy of *How to Talk to a Broker*, by Jay J. Pack. New York: HarperCollins, 1985.

Going It Alone

Once you have gained some feeling for the market, you may want to plunge right in and do your own stock selection. If you decide to follow this course, you must be prepared to regard it as a learning experience, for *it is very unlikely you will pick all winners*—even the pros don't manage to do that. So, at first, avoid putting more money than you can afford to lose in the market.

The best way to minimize your risks, of course, is to be well informed. To be your own broker you must be prepared to spend a significant amount of time reading about the economy and about individual companies, as well as the major industries.

Where You Can Find Information

1) *Specialized financial periodicals and newspapers* are excellent sources of information on the general economic climate and the stock market. In particular: *Barron's, The Wall Street Journal, The New York Times,* and *The Chicago Tribune* among the newspapers. Good magazines are: *Forbes, Business Week, Your Money, Fortune, U.S. News,* and *Money.* We have mentioned previously *Better Investing,* the monthly magazine of the National Association of Investment Clubs. Devoted to investment education, it analyzes stocks and covers various views on investments.

2) *Brokerage firms have a wealth of research material.* The large houses will send you some material, even if you are not a customer—at least for a limited period. Many have copies of newsletters on display in their retail offices. Although much of this information is generally known, you can still gather ideas, and certainly it is valuable for background data.

3) *Annual reports of corporations are an important source.* Write or call any company you are considering investing in and ask for a copy. Then read the section in this book called "How to Read an Annual Report" in the appendix.

4) *Standard & Poor's Stock Reports,* is regarded as a bible in the financial world. It contains one page, both sides, on each company listed on the NYSE. S&P also publishes similar volumes for the American Stock Exchange and for over-the-counter stocks. The material is revised periodically. For each corporation you will find a summary description, the current outlook, and new developments, plus a ten-year statistical table.

5) *Standard & Poor's Stock Guide* is a small monthly booklet containing basic data in condensed form on 5,100 stocks: price range, P/E ratio, dividend history, sales, an abbreviated balance sheet, earnings, and the S&P rating. A similar monthly booklet is put out covering bonds. For further details on all S&P publications, contact:

Standard and Poor's Corporation
25 Broadway
New York, NY 10004
212-208-8000 or, 800-221-5277

6) Value Line Investment Survey contains the most comprehensive coverage of stocks. Value Line follows 1,700 companies and their industries. Each industry is updated quarterly. Stocks are ranked on the basis of timeliness for purchase and safety. A subscription to this service also includes a separate weekly analysis of the market and general economic situation plus an in-depth discussion of one stock recommended for purchase. Contact:
Value Line, Inc.
220 East 42nd Street
New York, NY 10017
800-833-0046

7) *Financial newsletters can be helpful, but they vary enormously in reliability and success as far as their advice goes.* Before subscribing to any newsletter, try to locate copies at your library or by contacting the publisher. Many will send a free copy or offer trial subscriptions at a reduced rate.

There is also a service that rates the advisors. *Hulbert Financial Digest* is a monthly newsletter that tracks and ranks 160 of the stock market newsletters based on their performance in recommending stocks. One issue costs $15; a five-month subscription is $37.50; a full year's subscription is $135. Contact: Hulbert Financial Digest, 316 Commerce Street, Alexandria, VA 22314; 703-683-5905.

8) *Sale and purchase of a company's stock by officials of the corporation is one way to determine trends in the price of the stock.* This information is given in *Value Line*.

9) If you have a computer and modem, you may want to take advantage of the many on-line services which provide basic information such as current stock prices to more detailed information, including earnings and fast-breaking news about corporations.

For up-to-date information on what's available on-line, check out computer magazines which periodically offer round-ups on the best and most comprehensive financial and corporate information services as well as software. And, call several discount brokerage firms—most have reasonably priced on-line arrangements.

A Beginner's Stock Portfolio

- Abbott Laboratories
- American Home Products
- American Telephone & Telegraph
- Bristol-Myers Squibb
- CSX Corp.
- Emerson Electric
- General Electric
- Kellogg
- Mobil Corp.
- Pacific Telesis
- PepsiCo
- Procter & Gamble
- Smucker
- Wrigley

Companies that Have Paid Dividends 50 Years or More

- American Brands
- American Home Products
- Bristol-Myers Squibb
- Duke Power
- Dun & Bradstreet
- DuPont
- Florida Progress
- GTE Corp.
- Kmart
- Kansas City Power & Light
- Morgan (J.P.)
- Peoples Energy
- Potlatch Corp.
- Stanley Works
- Washington Gas Light

Your Investment Achilles Heel

Even with rational research and thoughtful planning on your part, you may still fall prey to one or more of the ubiquitous emotional traps that lie in wait in the investment field.

Every investor has areas of vulnerability. If you recognize yours, it's possible to eliminate many errors and reduce misjudgments. Here are the five most common pitfalls small investors should avoid when buying and selling stocks.

1) Tendency to hold on to securities too long, hoping a poor performer will turn around
2) Reacting immediately to bad news and selling too soon
3) Refusing to sell and take the profit because you feel you can squeeze out a few more points
4) Refusing to take a profit because of capital gains tax, even when the stock is fully valued
5) Avoiding selling a stock you inherited because of sentimental feelings

One way to avoid these and other pitfalls is to have a game plan, to know what your financial objectives are and then stick to them.

SEVEN STOCK MARKET DO'S

1) Know whether you're investing for long-term appreciation or immediate income, and select stocks that match your goal.
2) If you're investing long term, remember that the market fluctuates daily and the item to focus on is earnings, not price.
3) Know about the industry. Don't purchase a medical technology stock or a high-tech issue without first studying the industry.
4) Read the company's annual and quarterly reports before buying stocks.
5) Stick with companies that are leaders within their industry.
6) Look for companies with proven records of consistent growth.
7) Be patient.

"DEAR SHAREHOLDER"

How to Read an Annual Report

Just looking at the pictures and skimming the headlines in an annual report won't really help you evaluate the investment potential of a company, but armed with a little knowledge ahead of time, you can glean a lot of useful material from even the thinnest report.

The typical annual report consists of a letter to the stockholders from the president or chairman, a description of the company's business operations, detailed financial tables, a mass of footnotes, and a statement by an outside auditor.

It's quite easy to get lost in this forest of financial statistics, yet by developing your own search system—one that can be used with any annual report—you will soon have a basic comprehension of the business you may wish to invest in.

A word of caution: Don't let slick, glossy paper, artistic photographs, and two-tier pull-outs impress you unduly. These can be merely the work of a good public relations firm and not a true measure of the company. A simple presentation of the facts and an open divulging of financial statistics are what counts.

Step One

With an annual report, it's best to start at the back and review the material presented by the auditor-certified public accountant. This generally consists of a brief statement to the effect that the financial material was prepared in accordance with "generally accepted accounting principles" (GAAP). If that's it, then the company has been given a clean bill of health. If, however, the auditor's statement contains hedge clauses such as "the results are subject to," then beware. That's accountant-ese for an unresolved problem, perhaps a legal action that carries serious financial implications for the company. Frequently it implies that a ruling against the firm may lead to lower earnings than those printed in the annual report. Some statements are even less subtle: "Uncertainties exist as to the corporations's ability to achieve future profitable operations." All auditor's reservations should be noted before reading the rest of the annual report.

Step Two

At the beginning of nearly every annual report is the president's or chairman's letter to the stockholders. Traditionally this is management's chance to comment on last year's results and the outlook for the future. It also reflects the tone and direction of the company as viewed by management. Yet you should be aware of hidden caveats here, too: "All development went along as expected except for. . . " or, "We will meet our stated goals on target unless. . . ." think of these as warning signals. Approach the statement from management as an opportunity to learn how they think and plan.

Step Three

Footnotes come next. They often define terms and conditions actually used in the financial pages, such as a change in accounting methods. The footnotes will also alert you to the fact that earnings are up because of a windfall that won't occur again next year, or that legal action is pending.

Step Four

After you've waded through the footnotes, turn to the income statement, usually located in the middle of the report. It will give you a good idea of what directions sales and earnings took during the year as compared with the previous year. If both earnings and sales went up during the year, it certainly is good news. It's even better if earnings rose faster than sales. The income statement also gives you a picture of the company's cash flow position. Cash flow consists of net profits plus depreciation. To arrive at a measurement of cash flow, divide the cash flow figure found in the statement by the amount of long-term debt. Anything under 20 percent is generally regarded as unsuitable—although there are exceptions.

Step Five

You should now turn to the profitability of the company. The margin of profit is determined by taking the operating income (i.e., income before payment of income tax) and dividing it by total sales. Certain industries, such as supermarket chains, have low profit margins—1 percent to 2 percent—whereas most industrial companies have margins in the neighborhood of 5 percent. Look for companies with stable and rising profit margins.

Step Six

The balance sheet, traditionally a two-page spread, contains the company's assets (everything the company owes) on the right. Things that can quickly be converted into cash are called current assets, while the debts due within one year(which can be paid out of current assets) are called current liabilities. It is important to realize that the balance sheet offers the company's financial picture only at a single point in time. Like a snapshot, it gives you an instant idea of the corporations's strength. It's purpose is to show what the company owes and owns. Among the things to check are:

- How much cash is included under current assets. If the amount is shrinking, you must question what is draining this money from operations.
- The next working capital figure, a key number in determining a company's financial health. You can calculate this by subtracting current liabilities from current assets. This is what actually would be left over if all current debts were paid off; therefore it shows the resources available within the company to cover short-term debts. You can determine if this dollar amount is at a safe level by converting it into a ratio. Simply divide current assets by current liabilities to get the current asset-to-debt ratio. Most stock analysts like to see a 2:1 ratio. The net working capital is a crucial figure for investors to monitor, for if it drops there may not be sufficient money for expansion of future growth.
- The quick ratio, another means of determining financial strength, can be derived from the balance sheet. To arrive at this number, subtract inventories from current assets and divide by current liabilities. This figure should be more than one; in other words, current assets less inventories should at least be equal to if not greater than current liabilities. The quick ratio is a way to find out if a company is able to take care of its current debts as they mature.
- The company's ability to meet its obligations is another measure of financial strength. This, too, can be determined from the balance sheet by finding the debt-to-equity ratio. Divide long-term debt by total capitalization; both figures are generally given. (Total capitalization; consists of long-term debt, common stock, capital surplus, retained earnings, and preferred stock.) A manufacturing company is in good shape if debt is 20 percent or less of

capitalization. Higher debt ratios—40 percent to 50 percent—are acceptable in some industries, such as utilities. A high debt-to-equity ratio indicates that the company is probably borrowing to keep going—an acceptable position if sales are growing too and if there is an adequate amount of cash to meet payments. Beware, however, if sales start to fall.

There are many more sophisticated ratios you can obtain from working with the annual report, but these six steps are a good beginning. Don't forget to look for the elementary facts, too. They're just as important and include:

- The size of the company. What are its assets? A large company is less likely to face a sudden failure.
- The age of the company. Older firms have weathered good times and bad.
- The management. Are they experienced and are they personally investing in the company?
- The company's earnings. Are net earnings per share going up? Check the previous five years' record and look for trends in net sales, too.

There are other important indicators in the annual report. So for more extensive instruction on how to make sense out of the report, contact any Merrill Lynch Pierce Fenner & Smith office and ask for a copy of "How to Read a Financial Report." The important thing to keep in mind is that you must compare these key indicators from one year to the next. Is the company's net working capital up or down? What is the trend in the changes in the debt-to-equity ratio? One year's statistics are not sufficient evidence on which to judge a company.

Nine Easy/Painless Ways to Save

Granted, it's a great deal more fun to spend money on a romantic dinner in a restaurant or for a winter vacation in the Caribbean, yet to make certain you can always dine out and travel in style, you need to save. Extra dollars not only make dreams come true, they also let you sleep at night. If you want college for your kids, a house of your own, and a retirement nest egg, build your savings by following these nine easy tips. You'll find saving is infectious.

1) **Make savings your first bill.** Once a month when you pay your bills, write a check to deposit in your money market fund or savings account at your bank or credit union. Start by saving 1 percent of your take-home pay the first month; then increase the amount by -1/2 percent each month. By the end of the year you'll be socking away 6-1/2 percent per month.

2) **Use automatic savings plans.** If you don't see it you won't spend it. Arrange for a certain amount—it can be as little as $50—to be taken out of your paycheck and automatically transferred to your savings or money market fund at a bank or credit union. Ask if your employer also has a payroll savings plan for E.E. Savings Bonds. **Alternatives:** Have your bank automatically transfer a certain amount from checking to savings each month; or have funds automatically withdrawn from your checking account and put in a money market fund.

3) **Leave credit cards at home.** Pay with cash or by check. You'll spend less and you'll avoid monthly interest charges on unpaid credit card balances.

4) **Defer taxes.** Money in an IRA, Keogh, 401(k), or other qualified retirement plan grows tax-free until withdrawn.

You can fund these plans by making small contributions several times a year rather than trying to pay in one large lump sum. **Alternatives:** Investments that are fully or partially tax exempt: municipal bonds, municipal bond mutual funds, EE Savings Bonds, and U.S. Treasury securities.

5) **Contribute to a stock purchase plan.** Many companies allow employees to contribute part of their salary to buy the firm's stock through automatic payroll deductions.

6) **Reinvest stock dividends.** See pages 45–46 for details.

7) **Keep making payments.** When you've paid off a mortgage or a loan, continue to write a check for the same amount (or at least half the amount) every month and put it into savings. You've learned to live without that money, so now you can sock it away.

8) **Save your change at the end of the day.** Small amounts add up quickly. Put your nickels, dimes, and quarters in a jar before going to bed.

9) **Treat yourself.** Saving is smart but not always immediately gratifying. The payoff is sometimes several years away. Now and then spend a little on yourself. It will make saving much easier.

INDEX

About the Author

Nancy Dunnan is a financial analyst. She hosts a regular call-in program on public radio in New York and appears regularly on CNN. In addition to *How to Invest $50 to $5,000*, she is the author of *Dun & Bradstreet Guide to $Your Investments$®*, *Your First Financial Steps*, and *How to Make Money Investing Abroad*. She writes a monthly column, "Question & Answers," for *Your Money* magazine.

Dunnan was awarded the Distinguished Service Award in Investment Education from the Investment Education Institute, an affiliate of the National Association of Investors Corporation. A native of Ft. Dodge, Iowa, she lives in Manhattan.